Nick Nairn's Top 100 Salmon Recipes

To my best friend and wife, Holly

Food photography by Philip Webb

Nick Nairn's Top 100 Salmon Recipes
Original edition © 2002 by Nick Nairn 2002
The moral right of the author has been asserted.
First published in Great Britain by BBC Worldwide
Ltd. 80 Wood Lane, London W12 0TT
North American edition © 2002 by Winding Stair Press
Food photography © BBC Worldwide

Winding Stair Press
An imprint of Stewart House Publishing Inc.
290 North Queen Street, #210
Etobicoke, Ontario, M9C 5K4
Canada
1-866-574-6873
www.stewarthouse.com

National Library of Canada
Cataloguing in Publication Data
Nairn, Nick
  Nick Nairn's top 100 salmon recipes :
  quick and easy dishes for every occasion
North American ed.
Includes index.
ISBN 1-55366-260-1
1. Cookery (Salmon) I. Title. II. Title: Top 100 salmon
recipes. III. Title: Nick Nairn's top one hundred salmon
recipes
TX748.S24N33 2002   641.6'92   C2002-900535-3

Executive Vice President and Publisher: Ken Proctor
Director of Publishing and Product Acquisition: Joe March
Production Manager: Ruth Bradley-St-Cyr
North Americanization: Alison Maclean and Laura Brady
Commissioning Editor: Nicky Copeland
Project Editor: Sarah Miles
Copy-editor: Rachel Connolly
Cover Art Director: Pene Parker
Book Designer/Photo Art Director: Lisa Pettibone
Home Economist: Maxine Clark
Stylist: Helen Trent

This book is available at special discounts for bulk pur-
chases by groups or organizations for sales promo-
tions, premiums, fundraising and educational purpos-
es. For details, contact: Stewart House Publishing Inc.,
Special Sales Department, 195 Allstate Parkway,
Markham, Ontario L3R 4T8. Toll free 1-866-474-3478.

1 2 3 4 5 6 07 06 05 04 03 02

Many thanks to Nicky Copeland at BBC Books for
starting off this project and keeping me focused, also
to her team, Sarah Miles, Pene Parker and Lisa
Pettibone for making it as painless as possible. Special
thanks to Maxine Clark for inspiration, recipe tasting
and her help in styling the food for the photography,
also to Nadine Carmichael, my 'assistant', for the con-
siderable time, effort and good humor she put into
this book. A big thank you to Philip Webb for some
wonderful photographs and last, but not least, to Nick
Meakin of Aquascot, for his vision, support and com-
mitment to producing top quality salmon.

nick nairn's top **100**

Salmon recipes

Quick and easy dishes for every occasion

WINDING STAIR PRESS

Contents

Introduction

Why salmon?

Whether making a meal at home or working in a restaurant, Scottish salmon is my favorite fish to cook. I don't think that any other fish is quite as versatile – salmon can be cooked in many different ways and goes well with so many different ingredients. The hardest part of writing this book wasn't coming up with 100 salmon recipes, but deciding which ones to leave out.

In many ways, salmon is the ultimate fast food as it is so quick and easy to prepare. For some of the recipes in this book, it takes less than ten minutes from unwrapping the salmon to serving it up as a complete meal. When I'm feeling peckish, for example, my Lemon Butter Baked Salmon with Tagliatelle and Parsley (see page 76) can go from fridge to fork, all in the time it takes to cook the pasta. Now that's real fast food.

Salmon is currently the most popular fish on sale in supermarkets in the United Kingdom, and it is easy to see why. You'll find ready skinned and boned packs of fillets that are easy to use, consistently tasty and require zero preparation – perfect for those with a busy lifestyle. Serve salmon at your dinner party and your guests will feel truly pampered, yet it's also perfect as a family lunch or speedy supper without having to worry about breaking the bank.

A balanced diet is every bit as important as preparation time and budget, and salmon comes out top here, too. It's a fantastic source of omega-3 fatty acids, which can help prevent heart disease, and is a tasty provider of protein as well. It also lends itself perfectly to health-conscious cooking methods: steaming, poaching and grilling are all simple ways to retain the subtle sea-like flavor of salmon. To be honest, all you really need is a frying pan and a drizzle of sunflower oil.

Farmed salmon or wild salmon?

Fifteen years ago, there was plenty of wild Scottish salmon available and it was a natural product, caught by Scottish fishermen. Around the mid-eighties, the stocks of the fish began to decline, probably as a result of both changing climate conditions and unscrupulous offshore netting.

This led to a shortage of wild salmon, and as a consequence, salmon farming increased dramatically off the west coast of Scotland. Initially, the quality of this salmon was not as good as wild salmon, but it quickly improved. Like any type of farming, the good farmers produced great products; the salmon from farms in Shetland stood out in particular. These farmers situated their salmon pens in areas with a high tidal flow, they did not overcrowd their pens, and they did not try to force the fish to mature as quickly as possible. Instead, their salmon grew naturally, were fed only when they needed to eat and, within about eighteen months, grew into mature salmon. The quality was excellent, the price was stable and the salmon was available virtually all year round. Everyone was happy.

Around about 1986, as wild salmon became both scarcer and more expensive, I had started using farmed Shetland salmon in my first restaurant and by 1990, I was using nothing but, because it was such a good product. Then it all started to go wrong.

Between 1990 and 1995, the quality of Scottish farmed salmon went into decline. It transpired that many of the Scottish salmon farmers had tried to make their product compete as a commodity in the global marketplace. For various reasons, countries such as Chile and Norway could produce farmed salmon more cheaply than the Scots, and rather than competing as a premium quality product, Scottish farm salmon was trying to compete on price. Quantity rather than quality became the driving force. Intensive rearing practices had disastrous consequences on the salmon's texture and taste, as well as causing knock-on environmental problems.

I was concerned. Scotland's natural larder has an enviable reputation that poorly farmed salmon was beginning to tarnish. Around that time, I started working as a consultant with a salmon feed company. They realized that unless the situation improved, the Scottish salmon farming industry was in danger of disappearing, and with it their market for salmon feed. So they bought a number of fish farms on Orkney and started to reintroduce high farming standards. They believed that farmed Scottish salmon should not compete with other countries on price; it should compete on quality and be at the top end of the market. Scotland's natural sea resources provided the perfect environment to do just this.

At the time of writing, I do not believe that we have quite reached the standard of the best farmed salmon of twelve years ago, but we are making vast progress and good-quality Scottish salmon is now generally available at a reasonable price. One of the most exciting advances for me has been the development of organic Orkney salmon by Aquascot Seafarms, the sponsors of this book, who supply all the major supermarkets with top quality fish. I think this is as close as farmed salmon has got to the quality of wild fish.

Boding well for the future of the Scottish salmon industry, organic Orkney salmon is fetching a substantial premium over conventionally farmed salmon. My hope for the Scottish salmon industry is that companies such as Aquascot will up the game for everybody else. When other farmers see that it is possible to get a premium price for a premium product, then hopefully the whole industry will improve their standards. That way we can all benefit.

How to use this book

You've bought the salmon, so what should you do with it? The basic cooking techniques described in this book are easy, and the first recipe (see page 12) outlines simple instructions for perfectly cooked salmon. The rest of the book is intended as a source of inspiration. I love cooking salmon, and over the years I've experimented with countless ingredients and ideas; here I've brought you the best. Simple dishes stand side by side with exciting new recipe ideas, combining classic cooking techniques with a little imagination. I've also high-lighted the less obvious uses for salmon. Perhaps you've never made a salmon soup; if so, try my simple Hot-smoked Salmon Chowder (see page 34) and you'll be wondering why you never thought of it before.

Each recipe has been categorized, illustrating how easy it is to make, and whether it's best as an informal supper or to impress your dinner party guests. There's a guide to preparation time from start to finish, and each cooking stage is covered in easy-to-follow step-by-step instructions. For me, this is a book full of wonderful recipe revelations, simple and straightforward to use. I hope it will become a regular reference book in your kitchen.

Buying salmon

Buying good-quality salmon is essential for these recipes. Quality salmon always has a nice gloss to its surface; avoid a dull fish at all costs and steer clear of loose, flabby flesh – the fillet should be firm and bright. All salmon has white fat lines, but these should be thin and not too dominant. Check for gaping in the flesh; mass-produced, badly farmed salmon has a flesh structure that is insufficiently developed to hold it together and it gapes open. Ask where it has come from. In terms of sea conditions, Orkney and Shetland are best, and Scottish is always preferable to Norwegian fish. Even if you're not planning on buying salmon, always have a look at what's on offer and you'll soon learn to distinguish the good from the bad. Practice makes perfect.

Most of us buy salmon as fillets or as a side of salmon. If you are buying a whole salmon, check for the same level of freshness that you would for any other fish. The salmon should have pink gills, clear bulging eyes as opposed to sunken cloudy eyes, and again the flesh should be springy. The scales should be bright, and if there is any odor at all, it should be of the sea rather than 'fishy.'

Smoked salmon

No fish is better suited to smoking than salmon. There are two types of smoked salmon: traditional smoked salmon, regarded by many as the most luxurious way to eat salmon, and hot-smoked salmon, sometimes called kiln roast salmon. Whichever type you try, it will only be as good as the salmon it is made from.

The traditional method of smoking salmon is to smoke it at a temperature of around 80°F for 6–12 hours. Originally a method of preserving fish, we now use smoking to give a delicious flavor to salmon. Smoked salmon should have a lovely melt-in-the-mouth texture and a good, strong, smoky flavor. It should not be chewy, but have a noticeably soft and yielding texture. I have included a number of recipes using traditionally smoked salmon in the book, but there is an awful lot to be said for the simplest way of serving this delicacy. Just slice it thinly, and arrange it on a plate with some good brown bread, butter, a wedge of lemon and lots of freshly ground black pepper.

Recently, hot-smoked salmon has become very popular. It is smoked at a much higher temperature than traditionally smoked salmon. The smoke doesn't just flavor the fish, it also cooks it and gives it a flaky texture. I'm a big fan of hot-smoked salmon, especially as it has different uses from traditionally smoked salmon. As it is cooked already, it is a good, flavorful ingredient to add in at the end of a recipe, as in my Hot-Smoked Salmon Kedgeree (see page 88).

Different cuts of salmon

Apart from the smoked salmon dishes, almost all the recipes within this book use one of four cuts of salmon: fillets, escalopes, medallions and darnes. Each cut is suited to certain dishes. I have recommended cooking methods for each dish, but do feel free to swap baking for poaching or steaming, and vice versa. Grilling and frying are also interchangeable, but I wouldn't recommend poaching or steaming either escalopes or medallions of salmon (see page 12 for cooking techniques).

Fillets of salmon should weigh about 140 g (5 oz) per portion. Baking is the most popular method of cooking fillets and is certainly one of the easiest. I actually prefer to fry salmon fillets in a heavy-based, non-stick frying pan, as this caramelizes the salmon's juices and produces a tastier fillet. Alternatively, fillets can be poached, steamed or grilled.

Escalopes are thick slices of fish with a strip of skin on one side. They're ideal for very fast frying and take at most two minutes to cook through. Fried skin-side-down, they have a lovely crispy surface with melting salmon underneath. Grilling will also deliver some of the same caramelized flavor and color but doesn't require any extra oil.

Medallions are meaty chunks of fish formed by cutting a side of salmon down the central fat line, then cutting across the two long strips. Again, these are best flash-fried, and can also be grilled.

A **darne of salmon** is a steak cut across the whole fish. Keeping the bone in the centre gives it some extra flavor when cooked. Darnes are good for steaming, poaching and baking, or can be fried or grilled.

Fillets

Fillets are formed by slicing a side of salmon across the way. A width of 5–8 cm (2–3 1/4 inches) should yield several 140 g (5 oz) portions.

Escalopes

For escalopes, you require a side of salmon with the pin bones removed but the skin still on. With a very sharp knife, cut 1.5–2 cm (about 3/4 inch) thick slices across the fish. Holding the knife at an angle of 45 degrees, cut from the flesh side through to the skin side.

Wines to drink with salmon

My favorite wines to accompany salmon vary with the style and weight of the particular dish. In general, however, my preferred grape variety is Chardonnay. I'd partner a fat Chardonnay from the New World with the robust Seared Salmon with Chili and Parmesan Polenta (see page 98) and a white burgundy with the more restrained flavors of Seared Salmon, Crushed Potatoes and Caviar Butter Sauce (see page 111). I'd also recommend Australian Riesling, especially from areas with a cool climate, like the Adelaide Hills. For those looking for unusual wine combinations, try an Australian Viognier or an Alsace Gewürztraminer, or perhaps a lightly chilled Pinot Noir, which would be especially good with Pancetta-wrapped Salmon with Mushroom and Barley Risotto (see page 90).

Cook's notes

I believe that you learn something every time you cook, and that the difference between professional chefs and home cooks is simply that the professionals have had a tad more practice. The more confidence you gain in the kitchen, the easier it all becomes. You learn that a roasting pan isn't just for roasting; you can cook with it on the stove-top. If you have a thermometer and a wok, you now have a deep fat fryer. Over time you'll find your own favorite kitchen essentials – I can't work without a good-quality, heavy cook's knife and always insist on a good set of heavy-based, stainless steel cookware. Add to that a heavy-based chopping board and you are in business. Next on my wish list is a colander, a set of stainless steel mixing bowls, a Drysak spatula (or good-quality fish slice), some spoonulas and a set of kitchen cutters. The same goes for ingredients – over the years I've tried almost every brand of storecupboard ingredient and now I stick to my favorites. A word on seasoning: I always season salmon *after* cooking, using Maldon sea salt, for its crunchy texture and iodine flavor, freshly ground black pepper and a squeeze of lemon juice. However, most of us have too much salt in our diet (it really is bad for you) and it's relatively easy to wean yourself off it. Beef up the lemon and black pepper and, in no time at all, I guarantee you'll start to taste the truer flavors of the food you're cooking.

Medallions

For medallions, take a whole side of skinless salmon and cut firmly through the fat line that runs down the back of the fish. This will give two long strips of salmon. Cut each of these into 2 cm (3/4 inch) slices.

Darnes

To make a darne of salmon, take a whole fish and cut it into 2.5 cm (1 inch) steaks across the fish.

1 Cooking Perfect Salmon

Quick and easy
Preparation time 5–10 minutes
Serves 4

4 × 140 g (5 oz) salmon fillets or steaks

freshly ground sea salt and freshly ground black pepper

a squeeze of lemon juice

One of the greatest attractions of salmon is how well it adapts to different cooking methods. Whether steamed, poached, grilled, baked, fried, smoked or eaten raw as sashimi (see page 67), each method produces different results in terms of texture and taste.

Whichever method you choose, it is vital not to overcook it. Really, it comes down to personal preference, but I believe that salmon should be served the same way as steak: medium rare. In practice, this means that the salmon should still be pink inside when it is served. To test, give it a gentle press or squeeze. Perfectly cooked salmon will give slightly, but not too much; if it's wobbly or jelly-like, then it's under-cooked. Salmon which is firm to the touch is definitely overcooked and you'll find eating it akin to chewing on cotton wool.

Baking Preheat the oven to 200°C/450°F. Dot the fillets with butter or drizzle with olive oil, season and place them on a greased baking tray. Put them in the oven for 7–8 minutes.

Char-grilling Using a ribbed cast-iron grill pan is the easiest way to recreate the charred smoky flavor of the barbecue. To prevent the salmon sticking to the pan, make sure you oil the salmon, not the pan, and don't be tempted to fiddle with the fillets while they're cooking. To form the characteristic 'stripes,' cook for 2–3 minutes on one side, then rotate the fish through 90 degrees and cook for a further 2 minutes. Repeat on the other side. Season and serve.

Grilling Preheat the grill to the highest setting. Line the grill pan with foil, dot the salmon with butter or drizzle with olive oil and grill for 2–3 minutes on each side. Season and serve.

Pan-frying/searing Heat a non-stick frying pan until *very* hot, then add a little sunflower oil. For thin cuts, fry the fillets for 2–3 minutes on each side, to get a caramelized crust; for thicker cuts, reduce to a medium heat once the salmon has been added, then cook for 5–7 minutes on one side and a further 2 minutes on the other side. Season and serve.

Poaching Fill a wide frying pan with water, just deep enough to cover the fillets. Once the water is barely simmering, poach the fish for about 5 minutes, until opaque and just set. Using flavored stock or even some lemon juice adds an extra dimension to the taste. For cold-poached salmon, slip the salmon into the simmering water, remove from the heat and leave to cool. The salmon will poach slowly in the cooling water. Season and serve.

Steaming This is the healthiest way to cook salmon. Throw some aromatic herbs, say tarragon or thyme, into the base of a steamer, add water and bring to the boil. Place the salmon, lightly oiled, into the steamer basket, put on the lid and steam for 5–8 minutes, making sure the steamer doesn't boil dry. Season and serve.

2 Pesto

Prepare in advance
Preparation time 15 minutes
Serves 6–8

2 garlic cloves, peeled

200 ml (3/4 cup) extra virgin olive oil

85 g (3 oz) fresh basil leaves (you really do need to weigh it)

50 g (6 tablespoons) pine nuts

50 g (1/2 cup) Parmesan cheese, freshly grated

freshly ground sea salt and freshly ground black pepper

I love the flavor of pesto, but unfortunately I've never tasted a decent shop-bought variety, so if you want the true flavor you'll have to make your own. If you have a food processor this is a fairly straightforward exercise. I recommend that you make a big batch and then freeze the pesto in an ice cube tray – turn out the pesto cubes, wrap them in plastic wrap and they keep for 6 months in the deep freeze. A word of advice: pesto should have a good, crunchy texture, so avoid overprocessing which produces a gluey texture. I don't mind the odd whole pine nut in pesto! A blob of pesto works a treat atop a baked fillet of salmon (see page 12).

1 Put the garlic and oil in the food processor and whizz until you've got a garlicky oil. Scrape down the side with a spatula, then add the basil and whizz until smooth.

2 Add the pine nuts and whizz for a few seconds until they start breaking down. Lastly, add the Parmesan and seasoning and process for a couple of seconds until mixed in. Scrape out into a clean jam jar, cover with a film of olive oil and keep in the fridge for up to 2 weeks, or freeze as suggested.

NB Each time you use some of the pesto from the jar, flatten down the surface with a spoon and splash in some more oil before returning to the fridge. This keeps the pesto sealed and stops it darkening and losing its freshness.

3 Sauce Vierge

Informal supper
Preparation time 15 minutes
Serves 4

125 ml (¹/₂ cup) olive oil

2 shallots, finely chopped or sliced

1 garlic clove, lightly crushed but still whole

4 ripe plum tomatoes, roughly chopped

2 tablespoons roughly chopped fresh basil

juice of ¹/₂ lemon

freshly ground sea salt and freshly ground black pepper

The posh name for virgin olive oil sauce, sauce vierge is essentially good-quality olive oil infused with Mediterranean flavors. I've tried many variations, but keep coming back to this recipe for its simple harmony of flavors. I love it served with a seared salmon fillet (see page 12).

As with all simple recipes, the quality of the raw ingredients is important, and here that means good-quality oil and ripe tomatoes. My current favorites are the small vine tomatoes or cherry plum tomatoes (pomodorini). In the restaurant we use fat plum tomatoes, and skin and de-seed them before dicing the flesh – a fiddly process that is more rewarding visually than to the taste buds. For home cooks, I recommend the more rustic approach of leaving the skin on and seeds in. Olive oil contains unsaturated fat, which means that it's healthier than butter sauce – but sadly still fattening if overindulged.

1 Place the olive oil, shallots and garlic in a small pan. Warm through over a gentle heat until the sauce is hot, but not boiling – you want to soften the shallots, not color them. Remove from the heat after 10 minutes and set aside. This can be made several days in advance and kept in the fridge.

2 When ready to serve, lift out the garlic clove, stir in the tomatoes, basil and lemon juice, return to the heat to warm through and season with salt and pepper.

4 Watercress Sauce

Low fat

Preparation time 10 minutes

Serves 4

2 × 100 g (3.5 oz) bags of washed watercress, heavy stalks removed

1 tablespoon butter

juice of 1 lemon

freshly ground sea salt and freshly ground black pepper

Watercress has a vivid peppery flavor that has a natural affinity with salmon. This is a low fat, tasty and healthy sauce; its only drawback is that it needs to be used shortly after making if you want to keep its intense green color, which looks so good with pink salmon, preferably poached (see pages 12–13).

1 Bring a large pan of salted water to the boil. Tip in the picked watercress and boil for 3 minutes. Using a slotted spoon, lift the watercress from the pan and put into a liquidizer.

2 Add 3–4 tablespoons of the cooking water, put on the lid and whizz for a couple of minutes until you have a smooth sauce (it may be necessary to add a little extra water). Add the butter and half the lemon juice and season with salt and pepper. Whizz again to incorporate the butter, check the seasoning, adding more lemon juice if necessary, and use straight away.

5 Green Mayonnaise

Quick and easy
Preparation time 5 minutes
Serves 4–6

175 g (6 oz) fresh mixed herbs

300 ml (1 1/4 cups) mayonnaise

freshly ground sea salt and freshly ground black pepper

Green Mayonnaise (or sauce verte) is a mixture of puréed herbs and mayonnaise. I use bought mayonnaise for this and my favorite variety is Hellmann's – use low fat only if you must. The choice of herb tends to be decided by availability, but in an ideal world it would be a mix of flat leaf parsley, chives and tarragon – perfect with poached or steamed salmon (see pages 12–13).

1 Pick over the herbs and strip the leaves from the stalks – you should end up with about 85 g (3 oz). Wash them and dry well on paper towel.

2 Put the herbs in a food processor and blitz well. Add the mayonnaise and blitz again, until smooth and creamy. Season to taste.

Variation
Classic sauce verte is made with watercress leaves or spinach – use 175 g (6 oz) watercress for this, leaves picked off, washed and dried, or the same amount of picked and washed spinach leaves – or a mixture of the two. You could even use rocket for a really peppery mayo.

6 Salsa Verde

Quick and easy
Preparation time 5 minutes
Serves 4–6

2 garlic cloves, finely chopped

freshly ground sea salt and freshly ground black pepper

4 anchovy fillets in oil, drained and rinsed (optional, but really make the sauce!)

3 tablespoons each chopped fresh parsley, mint and basil

1–2 tablespoons salted capers, rinsed and chopped

75 ml (1/3 cup) really good extra virgin olive oil

2 tablespoons lemon juice, freshly squeezed

This is a clean, sharp-tasting sauce that I find works best with seared salmon (see page 12). I like to use salted capers rather than brined ones, but they must be rinsed well to get rid of the salt. Capers are an acquired taste; if you've never tasted them before, now's the time to try – just pop one in your mouth, give it a good chew and savor that musky, exotic perfume that is unique to really good capers. The sauce is best used on the day of making but will keep for 2–3 days in the fridge.

1 Pound the garlic with a pinch of salt in a pestle and mortar until creamy. (You can also do this with the side of a knife, crushing the garlic gradually into the salt – use a piece of greaseproof paper to stop your chopping board smelling too much!)

2 Stir in the remaining ingredients and season with pepper. If not serving immediately, transfer to a jar and pour a layer of olive oil on top to exclude the air.

7 Butter Sauce

Quick and easy

Preparation time 6 minutes

Serves 4

2 tablespoons white wine

juice of 1 lemon

$^1/_2$ vegetable stock cube
(preferably Knorr)

1 tablespoon 35% cream
(optional)

225 g (1 cup) unsalted butter,
chilled and diced

freshly ground sea salt and
freshly ground black pepper

This is one of the most versatile sauces for salmon, as there is an almost infinite number of variations on the basic sauce. It is well worth the time and effort in learning to make a good butter sauce; the rich, buttery flavor, silky texture and tang of acidity make it the best friend to a nice piece of salmon, cooked any way you like (see pages 12–13). Unfortunately, it's not a sauce that can be reheated – the only way to make it in advance is to keep it in a thermos flask for up to 12 hours. It will sit in a small saucepan kept at the right temperature – 40–70°C (100–155°F) – for 2–3 hours (use a cooking thermometer if necessary). Covering the saucepan with plastic wrap will help to keep the heat in. Give it a quick whisk before serving.

1 Boil the white wine, lemon juice and stock cube together for 1 minute.

2 Stir in the cream, if using, add the butter and whisk madly over a low heat until the butter is amalgamated and the sauce slightly thickened. Season with salt and pepper and serve immediately.

NB The secret of trouble-free butter sauce is to keep the sauce at the right temperature. Too hot and the sauce will boil and split; too cold and the fat will set, again causing the sauce to split. To find the perfect temperature, it's best just to stick your finger in – it should feel warm, not hot.

Variations
Lemon Butter Sauce Add the finely grated rind of $^1/_2$ lemon to the wine, lemon juice and stock cube.
Chive (or Herb) Butter Sauce Add 2 tablespoons chopped fresh chives (or chervil, parsley, tarragon or dill) to the sauce at the end.
Caviar Butter Sauce Add 1 tablespoon caviar right at the end and serve immediately.

8 Hollandaise Sauce

Smart entertaining
Preparation 15 minutes
Serves 4

3 tablespoons water

3 egg yolks

juice of 1/2 lemon

1 tablespoon white wine vinegar

225 g (1 cup) unsalted butter, melted

a pinch of salt

a pinch of cayenne pepper

2 egg yolks

225 g (1 cup) hot melted butter

juice of 1 lemon

freshly ground sea salt and freshly ground black pepper

Hollandaise should be regarded as a special occasion sauce, partly because it requires a bit of effort with the whisk, and partly because the heavenly combination of egg yolks, butter and lemon produces a sauce which is on the sinful side of healthy. If you're short of time, you can try the quick version below. Using a blender, this has a lighter texture, which I sometimes think suits salmon better.

1 Place the water, egg yolks, lemon juice and vinegar into a heatproof bowl. Set over a pan of warm, not boiling, water and whisk the mixture with a fine wire whisk until it starts to thicken and the whisk leaves a visible trace in the mixture. This is hard work and will take about 5 minutes. Remove the bowl from the heat and keep warm.

2 Take the melted butter and, whisking continuously, pour a steady stream of butter into the cooked egg mixture. The butter must be poured at a speed that allows your whisking to absorb it into the egg mix, taking care not to let puddles form. If it gets too thick, add a tablespoon or two of hot water.

3 When all of the butter has been incorporated into the egg mixture, add the salt and cayenne pepper to taste. It may require another squeeze of lemon juice.

4 Keep the mixture warm – 40–70°C (100–155°F) – until required (use a cooking thermometer if necessary), but be warned – if the mixture is overheated or allowed to cool, the sauce will separate. If the mix does separate, it can easily be rescued by whisking the oily mess into a couple of fresh egg yolks and three tablespoons of hot water; in essence, treating the split mixture as the butter in stage **2**.

Variation

For a speedy version, put the egg yolks and 2 tablespoons boiling water into a liquidizer and place the lid on. Remove the center of the blender lid and cover the hole with a clean tea towel. Whizz for approximately 30 seconds until the yolks start to go fluffy. Pour the hot butter into the hole in a continuous stream (this should take 15–20 seconds). Add the lemon juice and some seasoning. Have a small Pyrex bowl ready, three-quarters full of boiling water. When the hollandaise is ready, pour out the water and pour in the hollandaise. Taste and adjust the seasoning. Covered in plastic wrap, the hollandaise will keep warm for about 1 hour (in a warm place!).

9 Peppered Salmon with Whisky Cream Sauce

Quick and easy
Preparation time 20 minutes
Serves 2

1 tablespoon black pepper-corns, crushed

$^1/_2$ tablespoon white pepper-corns, crushed

2 × 175 g (6 oz) salmon steaks or darnes (see pages 10–11)

1 level teaspoon Dijon mustard

freshly ground sea salt

15 g (1 tablespoon) butter

1 tablespoon whisky

150 ml ($^2/_3$ cup) 35% cream

1 tablespoon chopped fresh chives, plus extra to garnish

Unlike the other recipes in this section, this sauce is an integral part of the dish and is one of my favorite one-pan recipes. It has evolved from a peppered beef dish which I then adapted for chicken with great success, and it was only a matter of time before the curious cook in me tried it with salmon. The result? A very tasty dish indeed!

1 Mix together the crushed peppercorns. Smear the salmon steaks all over with the mustard and then press the peppercorns into the cut sides of the salmon – just enough to give it a nice thin coating. Season with salt.

2 Heat a frying pan until hot. Add the butter and, as soon as it starts to foam, lay in the salmon steaks. Reduce the heat to medium and fry the steaks for about 3 minutes on one side to brown them.

3 Turn up the heat, flip the steaks over, then splash in the whisky. Boil fast until the whisky has almost disappeared, then pour in the cream. Carefully scraping up any bits that are sticking to the bottom of the pan around the steaks, bring to a fast bubble.

4 Boil for 1–2 minutes until the sauce starts to thicken, then taste and season with more black pepper if necessary, and some salt. By this time the salmon should be just cooked – test with the tip of a knife; if it is still a wee bit pink, simmer over a low heat for a further minute. Stir in the chopped chives and serve immediately, garnished with the extra chives.

10 White Sauce

<table>
<tr><td>Prepare in advance</td></tr>
<tr><td>Preparation time 30 minutes</td></tr>
<tr><td>Serves 4–6</td></tr>
</table>

25 g (1 tablespoon) butter

25 g (¼ cup) flour

600 ml (2½ cups) milk

freshly ground sea salt and freshly ground black pepper

Béchamel or white sauce is considered by many people to be an old-fashioned, lumpy, stodgy sauce, more associated with school canteens than gastronomy. I, however, am a fan of a well-made white sauce. The secret of success lies in properly cooking the sauce – it needs at least 30 minutes to cook out the raw floury flavor – and keeping the dreaded lumps at bay. There are two weapons in the battle against lumps: the electric hand whisk and the sieve. Forcing a lumpy sauce through the sieve into a clean pan and then giving it a good thrash with the electric whisk will restore most lumpy disasters to silky smooth sauces.

Like butter sauce, white sauce is a great base to which to add flavors: cheese, mustard, chopped anchovies, herbs and cooked spinach being my most favored additions. These extras should be added at the end of the cooking time.

1 Melt the butter in a small, heavy saucepan. Add the flour and, using a wooden spoon, stir over the heat for a minute or so until you have a smooth paste.

2 Take the pan off the heat and, using a wire whisk, whisk in the milk all in one go. Make sure it is well blended.

3 Return to the heat and slowly bring to the boil, whisking all the time. Turn down the heat and simmer gently for 30 minutes, stirring occasionally to prevent a skin forming. Season to taste. This sauce can be cooled, covered and kept in the fridge and reheated (you may need to add a little more milk) when needed.

Variations

For a traditional béchamel sauce, heat the milk until just under boiling point, then add a couple of bay leaves, a blade of mace and half a raw onion. Leave to infuse for 20 minutes, then strain and make the sauce as in the recipe above.

Add 115 g (1 cup) strong grated Cheddar or Gruyère cheese and a little Parmesan if you like. A touch of Dijon mustard will lift it!

Add 2–3 tablespoons grain or Dijon mustard, depending on taste.

Add 4 tablespoons chopped fresh herbs.

Add 6 tablespoons chopped blanched spinach and a little freshly grated nutmeg.

Add 30 g (1 oz) canned anchovies, drained and chopped.

11 Red Wine Sauce

Quick and easy
Preparation time 10 minutes
Serves 4

150 ml (²/₃ cup) red wine

1 teaspoon soft dark brown sugar

300 ml (1 ¹/₄ cups) vegetable or fish stock

40 g (3 tablespoons) cold butter, diced

freshly ground sea salt and freshly ground black pepper

This is not a sauce that you would readily associate with salmon, but the tannin in the red wine gives the sauce an edge that helps cut the rich oiliness of salmon. A very easy-to-make sauce that works particularly well with seared salmon (see page 12).

1 Bring the wine to the boil in a saucepan, add the brown sugar and boil until it has reduced by about three-quarters to form a thick and foamy syrup.

2 Add the stock and boil until reduced to about 150 ml (²/₃ cup), then whisk in the diced butter a few pieces at a time, swirling the pan as the butter melts. The sauce needs to be dark and glossy, so don't use a hand blender to whisk in the butter as this would make it too foamy. Keep swirling until the butter has been incorporated, then season and serve immediately.

NB You can make the sauce in advance – just don't add the butter until right before serving.

12 Smoked Salmon and Rocket Rolls

Quick and easy
Preparation time 5 minutes
Serves 4

4 tablespoons best fruity olive oil

1 tablespoon lemon juice or balsamic vinegar

8 slices of smoked salmon

40 g (1 ¹/₂ oz) rocket

1 tablespoon freshly grated Parmesan cheese

2 tablespoons pine nuts, toasted

freshly ground sea salt and freshly ground black pepper

These couldn't be simpler to prepare, and the peppery flavor of rocket works particularly well with the smoky salmon. They also make a nice starter for a dinner party, as you can prepare the rolls up to an hour in advance. Use the best olive oil you can find.

1 Mix the oil with the lemon juice or balsamic vinegar.

2 Lay out the smoked salmon on a board and spread the rocket on top. Scatter over the Parmesan and pine nuts, drizzle with a few drops of the oil mixture, then season and roll up (you could always fold them into little parcels – easier to eat, but not so nice to look at!).

3 Drizzle around the remaining oil mixture and serve.

Variations
Use watercress instead of rocket for an equally peppery taste.
Add sliced mozzarella cheese to the rolls with the rocket, and miss out the Parmesan.
Cut up char-grilled artichokes (buy these in oil from good Italian delis) and add them to the rolls with all the rest.
The important thing is to get the right balance of freshness, sharpness, crunch and sweetness.

13 Smoked Salmon, Cream Cheese and Black Pepper Roulades

Smart entertaining
Preparation time 15 minutes plus chilling time
Makes about 10

85 g (6 tablespoons) cream cheese (preferably Philadelphia or you could use Welsh goats' cheese instead)

freshly ground sea salt and freshly ground black pepper

5 slices of smoked salmon

freshly squeezed lemon juice

Smoked salmon has a natural affinity with cream cheese – as seen in the smoked salmon and cream cheese bagel, one of the best-selling sandwich combos in the world. The addition of liberal quantities of black pepper puts a bit of spice into these tasty treats. They are more robust than dainty – at least two bites in each; if you want dainty, then cut each roll in two.

1 Beat the cream cheese with a little salt and lots of freshly ground black pepper.

2 Spread the cheese thinly over the salmon slices and add a touch of lemon juice. Cut each salmon slice in half widthways to give two pieces. Roll up, starting at the cut edge. Wrap in plastic wrap and chill for 1 hour.

3 Sprinkle a little coarsely ground pepper on a plate. Unwrap the salmon rolls and lightly coat each one in the pepper, shaking off the excess. Trim off one edge of each roll and stand up on the cut edge. Arrange on a plate and serve.

14 Smoked Salmon and Couscous Sushi

Prepare in advance
Preparation time 30 minutes
Makes about 12–15

finely grated rind of 1 lemon

a squeeze of lemon juice

130 ml (1/2 cup) chicken, vegetable or fish stock

freshly ground sea salt

115 g (3/4 cup) quick-cook couscous

3 tablespoons chopped fresh coriander

3 sheets of nori seaweed (pre-toasted)

soy sauce and Japanese pickled ginger, to serve

FOR THE FILLING:

1/2 good-sized cucumber

1 teaspoon wasabi (fiery Japanese horseradish)

a small bunch of long chives

225 g (8 oz) sliced smoked salmon

From left: Hot-smoked Salmon Potatoes with Crème Fraîche and Chives, Crostini of Smoked Salmon, Avruga and Quail's Eggs and Smoked Salmon and Couscous Sushi

I love sushi, but preparing the rice is a bit of a palaver – all that washing and fanning takes ages. If you replace the rice with couscous it becomes much easier and quicker to make. I have to give due credit to John Webber for this recipe. John runs my cookery school and, as well as being a superb tutor, he is a constant source of ideas and information.

1 First, prepare the filling. Take the cucumber and cut into a length the same width as the nori. Cut lengthways into slices 5 mm (1/4 inch) thick, then cut the slices into batons the same thickness. Smear the entire length with wasabi.

2 Lay 4 or 5 long chives along the length of the batons and wrap in the sliced smoked salmon. Cover and refrigerate until required.

3 To cook the couscous, place the lemon rind, lemon juice, stock and a pinch of salt into a pan with a well-fitting lid. Bring to the boil. As soon as the stock has boiled, sprinkle in the couscous and stir. When the mixture starts to simmer, put on the lid and turn off the heat, leaving the couscous to absorb the hot stock. The couscous should be cooked after about 4 minutes – any longer and it will set like concrete! Fork up the couscous and fold in the coriander.

4 Lay a bamboo sushi mat on the table and place a sheet of nori on top, shiny side down. The mat should lie so that it rolls away from you not from side to side.

5 Spread a thin layer of the couscous on the seaweed, leaving about 3–4 cm (1 1/4–1 1/2 inches) of uncovered nori on the edge furthest from you (wet hands help here). Lay a strip of wrapped cucumber horizontally across and about one third of the way down the couscous. Use the bamboo mat to help you roll the nori and couscous around the filling so that it is fully enclosed, then moisten the uncovered strip of seaweed and complete the roll. The most difficult part of this is getting the roll tight enough to prevent it from disintegrating when it's sliced! If you have difficulty with the slicing, roll the sushi tightly in plastic wrap and refrigerate until needed.

6 Just before serving, use a sharp knife to cut each sushi roll into five pieces. Serve with soy sauce for dipping and Japanese pickled ginger.

15 Hot-smoked Salmon Potatoes with Crème Fraîche and Chives

Smart entertaining
Preparation time 25 minutes
Makes 20

10 even-sized small new potatoes

200 ml (7 fl oz) tub crème fraîche

115 g (4 oz) hot-smoked salmon, flaked

freshly ground sea salt and freshly ground black pepper

a small bunch of fresh chives

I make these delicious nibbles (see picture on page 29) only in the summer when you can get really good new potatoes. Supermarkets have finally cottoned on to the fabulous varieties available, and I've seen Anya, Charlotte and Ratte, as well as the more usual Jersey Royals and of course the fabulous Ayrshires. Take care when cooking new potatoes, as there is nothing worse than under- or overcooked potatoes.

1 Boil the whole potatoes in salted water for 15–20 minutes until tender. Drain, then place in a pan of cold water to cool them quickly.

2 When cold, drain again and pat dry. Cut each potato in half lengthways and shave a tiny slice off the rounded side of each half to act as a base – this will stop them rolling around the plate. Top the cut side of each potato half with a small spoonful of crème fraîche, place a good flake of hot-smoked salmon on top and season. Place a couple of snipped chives on top of each one, arrange on a plate and serve immediately.

16 Crostini of Smoked Salmon, Avruga and Quail's Eggs

Smart entertaining
Preparation time 25 minutes
Makes about 24

1 small, thin baguette

olive oil

1 teaspoon red or white wine vinegar

12 fresh quail's eggs, at room temperature

115–175 g (4–6 oz) sliced smoked salmon or smoked salmon pieces

1 × 55 g (about 2 oz) pot Avruga or Keta caviar or the real thing!

These crostini (see picture on page 29) are unashamedly posh nibbles for your best friends. The crunchy crouton, smoky salmon, salty Avruga and soft-boiled egg combo is delicious. The crostini can be made up to a week in advance and kept in an airtight tin. The only fiddly bit is shelling the quail's eggs. If you're really stuck for time you can buy jars of hard-boiled quail's eggs, but they're not a patch on the real thing.

1 To make the crostini, slice the baguette thinly into 24 slices and brush each side with a little olive oil. Place on a baking tray and bake at 180°C/350°F for 5–10 minutes until crisp and golden. Remove, cool and store in an airtight tin.

2 Bring a pan of water to the boil and add the vinegar. Have a bowl of cold water handy. Place the quail's eggs in a blanching or french fry basket that fits into your pan. Gently lower the basket into the boiling water. Boil for 2 minutes, lift out and dunk into the cold water to stop them cooking.

3 Quickly peel the eggs under running water – this makes the peeling easier, as they are notorious for staying attached to their shells! (Also, if you let them get too cold, they are tricky to peel.) Then carefully cut the eggs in half lengthways.

4 To serve, top each crostini with a generous piece of smoked salmon. Place a very small spoonful of Avruga on top of the salmon and set half a quail's egg on top. Serve immediately.

17 Spicy Salmon Broth

Low fat
Preparation 20 minutes
Serves 4

1 tablespoon vegetable oil

25 g (1 oz) fresh ginger, peeled and cut into matchsticks

2 large garlic cloves, peeled and sliced into slivers

1 large fresh red chili, seeded and cut into matchsticks

1 whole bird's eye chili

1 stem of lemon grass, chopped

1.2 liters (2 pints) chicken or vegetable stock

3 tablespoons Thai fish sauce (*nam pla*)

1 tablespoon light soy sauce (preferably Kikkoman's)

juice of 1 lime

4 green onions, finely shredded

175–225 g (6–8 oz) salmon fillet, cut into medallions (see pages 10–11)

3 tablespoons roughly chopped fresh coriander

freshly ground sea salt and freshly ground black pepper

I normally make this soup using a blend of fish stock and mussel juices; however, I know that most home cooks don't have ready access to that kind of kit, and so for this book I experimented using a fish stock cube – not great. I then tried my personal favorite, a Knorr chicken stock cube, and found that it made a really good soup, although perhaps not acceptable to 'pescatarians' (I know, it was a new one on me, too – it means fish-eating vegetarians!); alternatively you could use a vegetable stock cube. The base can be made in advance and freezes well. Add the salmon just prior to serving. Be careful not to overcook the salmon; it needs only a couple of minutes. You can check by breaking one of the pieces open – it should still be nice and pink inside.

1 Heat the oil in a large pan and add the ginger, garlic, chili and lemon grass. Cook over a low heat until softened.

2 Add the stock and splash in the Thai fish sauce, soy sauce and lime juice. Bring to the boil, then turn down the heat and simmer for 10 minutes. Add the green onions and cook for a further 3 minutes.

3 Add the fish with the coriander and simmer for 2 minutes or until the fish is cooked. Taste, season with salt and pepper and add more fish sauce or soy sauce if you like – it should be quite punchy! Ladle into warm bowls and serve.

18 Hot-smoked Salmon Chowder

Informal supper
Preparation time 30 minutes
Serves 4–6

50 g (¹/₄ cup) butter

225 g (1 cup) leeks, washed and sliced

450 g (1 lb) floury potatoes (such as King Edward), peeled and cut into large chunks

425 ml (1³/₄ cups) whole milk

300 ml (1¹/₄ cups) 18% cream

400 g (14 oz) hot-smoked salmon

2 tablespoons chopped fresh parsley

freshly ground sea salt and freshly ground black pepper

This is based on a traditional Scottish soup called Cullen Skink, normally made with smoked haddock, but I've had great success with hot-smoked salmon. Remember that, unlike ordinary smoked salmon, the salmon is already cooked so it only needs to be warmed through. This can be made in advance and reheats well, but it does not freeze.

1 Melt the butter in a saucepan and add the leeks. Cook over a medium heat until starting to soften, then add the potatoes, milk and 425 ml (1³/₄ cups) water. Bring to the boil, then turn down the heat and simmer for 15 minutes until the potatoes start to disintegrate around the edges.

2 Add the 18% cream and heat thoroughly but don't boil. Skin and flake the salmon, then stir gently into the soup with the chopped parsley. Reheat and taste and adjust the seasoning – make it quite peppery!

19 Creamy Salmon and Asparagus Soup

Smart entertaining
Preparation time 25 minutes
Serves 4

700 g (1 lb 9 oz) fresh asparagus

50 g (1/4 cup) butter

1 large onion, finely chopped

225 g (8 oz) potatoes, peeled and finely sliced

1.2 liters (2 pints) light chicken or vegetable stock

1/2 teaspoon freshly ground sea salt

freshly ground white pepper

350 g (12 oz) salmon fillet, cut into 1 cm (1/2 inch) cubes

This soup is similar to the Spicy Salmon Broth (see page 32), in that chunks of salmon are cooked in a soup base; that way none of the flavor of the fish is lost, and you get a lovely contrast of textures – silky soup and chunky salmon. It also looks great and is reasonably healthy. Once again I recommend a Knorr chicken stock cube for the base.

1 Trim off any woody ends from the asparagus and, using a potato peeler, remove any tough skin layers. Cut off the top 4 cm (1 1/2 inches), including the tips, and blanch for 4 minutes in boiling salted water (allow four tips per person).

2 Remove from the water with a slotted spoon and refresh immediately in cold water. Drain and put to the side, retaining for a garnish. Roughly chop the remaining stalks.

3 Melt the butter in a large pan. Add the onion and potatoes and sweat down. Next, add the stock, bring to the boil and cook for 15 minutes or until the potatoes have broken down. Add the asparagus stalks and cook for 7 minutes until tender, then liquidize.

4 Return the soup to the pan, bring to the boil and reduce the heat, taste and season with salt and white pepper. Add the salmon chunks and simmer for 2 minutes.

5 Reheat the asparagus tips in boiling water and drain. Pour the soup into four bowls and garnish with the tips.

20 Smoked Salmon and Pea Soup

Prepare in advance
Preparation time 20 minutes
Serves 4

40 g (3 tablespoons) butter

1 medium onion, chopped

1 liter (1 3/4 pints) hot chicken or vegetable stock

450 g (1 lb) frozen peas, defrosted

2 tablespoons chopped fresh mint

freshly ground sea salt and freshly ground black pepper

225 g (8 oz) smoked salmon, cut into 1 cm (1/2 inch) cubes

extra cooked peas and sour cream or crème fraîche, to serve

Another soup where you make up the base in advance and add the smoked salmon at the last minute. I think the success of this soup lies in the combination of the sweet peas and the salty salmon. You can freeze this after the smoked salmon has been added, but prior to freezing do chill the soup as quickly as possible to keep its vivid color. I usually put the soup in a 2 liter (3 1/2 pint) jug and sit that in a sink of cold water, then add in some ice cubes if I have a tray spare.

1 Melt the butter in a deep saucepan. Add the onion and cook until it softens, taking care not to brown the onion or let the butter burn.

2 Add the hot stock and bring quickly to the boil. Add the peas and mint and simmer for 5 minutes, then remove from the heat and blitz in a liquidizer until smooth (unfortunately, a food processor isn't fast enough to produce the necessary smooth emulsion). Taste and season with salt and pepper.

3 Pour the soup into warmed bowls, add the salmon, then add the extra peas and sour cream or crème fraîche and serve.

21 Salmon Minestrone

Minestrone is one of my all-time favorite soups, and with the addition of some cubes of salmon it becomes an ideal one-pot lunch or supper dish. It's low in fat, has a good balance of carbohydrate, protein and vegetables, and it freezes well minus the salmon.

Informal supper
Preparation time 45 minutes
Serves 6

3 tablespoons olive oil

1 medium onion, chopped

1 leek, sliced

400 g (14 oz) can chopped tomatoes

200 g (7 oz) can navy beans, drained and rinsed

2 medium carrots, chopped

115 g (1 cup) potatoes, diced

a few sprigs of fresh thyme

2 bay leaves

225 g (8 oz) fresh or frozen peas, or green beans cut into short lengths

225 g (8 oz) zucchini, diced

225 g (8 oz) salmon fillet, cut into bite-sized chunks

freshly ground sea salt and freshly ground black pepper

3 tablespoons home-made Pesto (see page 13) or ready-made pesto (optional), and freshly grated Parmesan cheese, to serve

1 Heat the oil in a large pan, add the onion and leek and cook gently for 10 minutes until softened. Add the canned tomatoes and navy beans, the carrots, potatoes and herbs and cover with about 1.2 liters (2 pints) cold water. Bring to the boil, cover and simmer for 20–25 minutes until the beans and potatoes begin to disintegrate.

2 Add the peas or green beans and zucchini to the soup and simmer for 5 minutes, then add the salmon and cook for 3–4 minutes. Taste and check the seasoning.

3 Ladle the soup into warmed bowls and serve with a little pesto stirred in, if desired, and lots of grated Parmesan.

22 Salmon, Lemon and Saffron Soup

Smart entertaining
Preparation time 20 minutes
Serves 4

50 g (¹/₄ cup) butter

3 shallots, finely chopped

1 garlic clove, crushed

2 tablespoons flour

1 liter (1 ³/₄ pints) fish stock, or vegetable stock with a dash of Thai fish sauce (*nam pla*)

1 teaspoon saffron threads or strands

finely grated rind of 1 lemon and 1 lime

freshly ground sea salt and freshly ground black pepper

225 g (8 oz) salmon fillet, skinned and cut into large pieces

juice of ¹/₂ lemon and 1 lime

2 tablespoons roughly chopped fresh coriander

This sounds like quite an unusual combination, but the musky flavor of saffron with the citrus fruits produces a very clean-tasting soup with bags of flavor. It's important to use good-quality saffron – look for strands or threads rather than powder – as it has a much finer aroma. You could add a dash of green Tabasco to the soup for a wee kick!

1 Melt the butter in a large saucepan, add the chopped shallots and cook over a very low heat until soft and golden.

2 Stir in the garlic and flour, turn up the heat and cook for 1 minute.

3 Take the pan off the heat and whisk in the fish stock. Return to the heat and bring slowly to the boil, stirring continuously – this way you won't get any lumps!

4 Add the saffron and lemon and lime rind and season with the salt and pepper. Pop a lid on and simmer for 10 minutes.

5 Add the chopped salmon, reduce the heat and cook for a further 2 minutes or until the fish is cooked (it should be opaque and firm).

6 Add the lemon and lime juice to taste. Check the seasoning and add the coriander. Ladle into warmed bowls.

23 Smoked Salmon and Parmesan Cream Soup

Quick and easy

Preparation time 10 minutes

Serves 6

600 ml (2 1/2 cups) 35% cream

150 ml (2/3 cup) hot vegetable stock or water

6 tablespoons grated Parmesan cheese

175 g (6 oz) smoked salmon, roughly chopped

freshly squeezed lemon juice

freshly ground sea salt and freshly ground black pepper

extra finely shredded smoked salmon, to serve

This is a very rich, intensely flavored soup, which I wouldn't recommend as part of a calorie-controlled diet. But it is super-tasty, and as a little of what you fancy does you good, I sometimes serve this in small coffee cups. Just before serving, give the soup a good old froth up with an electric hand blender to lighten the texture.

1 Pour the cream and stock into a medium-heavy saucepan and stir in the Parmesan. Slowly bring to the boil, stirring from time to time. When it's just beginning to boil, whip it off the heat, cool for a minute and pour into a liquidizer.

2 Add the smoked salmon and give it a good blitz until smooth. Season with a squeeze or two of lemon juice, a little salt (the smoked salmon and Parmesan are already quite salty) and lots of black pepper.

3 Pour into warmed coffee cups or small soup bowls and garnish with extra shredded smoked salmon.

24 Grilled Salmon with Pea Purée

Informal supper
Preparation 20 minutes
Serves 4

300 ml (1 1/4 cups) 35% cream

225 g (1 1/2 cups) frozen peas

freshly ground sea salt and freshly ground black pepper

4 × 140 g (5 oz) salmon fillets

olive oil, for brushing

Frozen peas make an excellent purée and this recipe couldn't be easier. The purée is rather rich, so you don't need any extra sauce, which helps to justify the amount of cream used. It's a pretty dish, with the vivid green of the purée enhancing the pink of the salmon. I like to serve baby new potatoes and some dressed salad leaves on the side.

1 Bring the cream to the boil, add the peas and simmer for 6–7 minutes until tender, then tip into a blender or liquidizer. Add salt and pepper to taste and whizz until smooth. The purée shouldn't be too thick; a sign that it is too thick is when it sticks to the sides of the liquidizer – add a little more cream or milk to loosen it.

2 Heat a grill pan. Brush the salmon fillets with a little olive oil and place into the pan. After 2 minutes turn through 90 degrees, cook for another 2 minutes, turn over and repeat. There should be nicely criss-crossed grill marks on the salmon.

3 Spoon the purée on to four plates, and serve with a piece of salmon on top.

25 The Ultimate Salmon Sandwich

Quick and easy
Preparation time 5 minutes
Serves 2

4 slices of your favorite bread

butter, softened

3 medium-sized vine tomatoes

175 g (6 oz) poached or cooked salmon (see pages 12–13)

lemon juice

1 heaped tablespoon mayonnaise

freshly ground sea salt and freshly ground black pepper

rocket leaves or watercress

This may not be the kind of recipe that you'd expect in a book like this, but after the photo shoot for the book, we had loads of cooked salmon left over and I made these sandwiches for everyone's lunch. They were universally declared to be the best salmon sandwiches ever, and the recipe *had* to go in the book! So here it is.

1 Butter the slices of bread. Halve the vine tomatoes, squeeze out the tomato water and seeds, cut each half into three, then cross-cut into nine – essentially you are roughly chopping the toms, but in a quick and neat way!

2 Flake the salmon, squeeze over a little lemon juice and mix in the tomatoes, mayonnaise, salt and pepper.

3 Pile the salmon mix on two slices of bread, then top with some rocket and the remaining bread. Press down lightly to flatten a bit, cut in two, and eat right away.

26 Salmon Rillettes

Prepare in advance
Preparation time 30 minutes plus chilling time
Serves 4

350 g (12 oz) salmon fillet

juice of $1/2$ lemon

115 g ($1/2$ cup) butter, softened

$1/4$ teaspoon ground mace

$1/4$ teaspoon ground allspice

freshly ground white pepper

2–3 tablespoons chopped fresh mixed herbs (chives, parsley and tarragon)

freshly ground sea salt

Salmon rillettes are a real classic, not unlike potted shrimps. To 'pot' any meat or fish, you need to pound it with a good amount of butter and spices. The secret is not to add too much butter or it can become cloying. Try to find ground mace – there's nothing quite like its delicate flavor, and it goes particularly well with salmon.

1 Poach the salmon fillet (see pages 12–13), using half the lemon juice. Remove the pan from the heat and let the fish cool in the liquid. By the time the liquid is cold the salmon will be perfectly cooked and still moist in the middle. When cold, lift the salmon out of the pan, drain well and put in a bowl.

2 Cream the soft butter with the mace, allspice, white pepper and chopped mixed herbs, then whisk in the remaining lemon juice.

3 Shred the salmon roughly and fold into the flavored butter without breaking it up too much – you want to retain that rough texture. Taste and season with salt and white pepper. Pack into ramekins, cover and chill until needed.

4 Remove from the fridge for 30 minutes to allow the rillettes to reach room temperature before serving with hot toast and a bit of chutney or onion marmalade.

27 Seared Salmon Oriental Salad with Sweet Chili Dressing

Low fat
Preparation time 20 minutes
Serves 4

4 × 115 g (4 oz) salmon escalopes (see page 10)

freshly ground sea salt and freshly ground black pepper

a squeeze of lemon juice

FOR THE ORIENTAL SALAD:

1 mango, peeled, pitted and diced

85 g (^{3}/$_4$ cup) fresh beansprouts

1 carrot, finely shredded into ribbons (use a potato peeler)

1 big juicy red chili, finely shredded

50 g (2 oz) mizuna or watercress

25 g (1 oz) fresh coriander

2 tablespoons roughly chopped cashew nuts

1 tablespoon sesame seeds

FOR THE SWEET CHILI DRESSING:

4 tablespoons rice wine vinegar

4 tablespoons light sesame oil

4 tablespoons sweet chili sauce

This dish has everything going for it – a great combo of flavors and textures, and it looks good. The dressing is easy to prepare and keeps for several weeks in the fridge. I store mine in a plastic squeezy bottle which makes it perfect for instant 'drizzling' round the edge of plates.

1 Mix the salad ingredients together, season and set aside.

2 Mix the dressing ingredients together and set aside.

3 Fry the salmon escalopes for 1–2 minutes over a searing heat, turn out on to a plate cooked-side up and season with salt, pepper and a squeeze of lemon juice.

4 Dress the salad leaves with a tablespoon of the sweet chili dressing. Ensure that the leaves are simply coated rather than left in a pool of dressing. Divide the salad between the serving plates, gently place the seared salmon on top, spoon around the remainder of the sweet chili dressing and serve.

28 Hot-smoked Salmon with Avocado Salsa

Smart entertaining
Preparation time 25 minutes
Serves 4

115 g (4 oz) baby salad leaves

50 ml (¹/₄ cup) good olive oil

a squeeze of lemon juice

freshly ground sea salt and freshly ground black pepper

225g (8oz) hot-smoked salmon, flaked into large pieces

FOR THE SALSA:

1 large ripe avocado

2 ripe plum tomatoes, peeled, seeded and chopped into 1 cm (¹/₂ inch) dice

¹/₂ red onion, finely chopped

1 fresh red chili, seeded and finely chopped

1 tablespoon finely chopped Japanese pickled ginger

2 tablespoons chopped fresh coriander

2 teaspoons Thai fish sauce (*nam pla*)

juice and grated rind of 1 lime

a pinch of freshly ground sea salt

FOR THE BALSAMIC SYRUP:

300 ml (1 ¹/₄ cups) balsamic vinegar

This is one of my most tried and tested starters – it's perfect as a dinner party opener for a large number of guests, as all the prep is done in advance. The biggest number I've prepared for at one time is 600, for the dinner to celebrate the opening of the Scottish Parliament.

I like to mold this into a neat tower using a scone cutter (straight sides, not fluted), but you can use any kind of mold – I've used bits of drainpipe, even a yoghurt carton with the bottom snipped off.

1 To make the salsa, halve the avocado and remove the pit. Halve again and remove the skin before chopping it into 1 cm (¹/₂ inch) chunks. Place in a mixing bowl and add the other salsa ingredients. Mix well and leave at room temperature for about 10 minutes for the flavors to develop.

2 Lightly dress the salad leaves in a teaspoon of olive oil, a small squeeze of lemon juice and a pinch of seasoning.

3 Place the chosen mold in the center of a plate and fill it half full with the flaked salmon. Lightly press down. Fill to the top with the salsa and gently press down. Lift off the ring and top with a small pile of salad leaves. Drizzle the balsamic syrup around the plate, then drizzle with some olive oil. Alternatively place a generous helping of the salsa in the center of each serving plate and top with the hot-smoked salmon. Arrange a few salad leaves on top and then drizzle the balsamic syrup and olive oil around the plate.

Balsamic Syrup
Reducing balsamic vinegar intensifies its flavor and makes it thick and syrupy. Ensure the kitchen is well ventilated, as the vinegary fumes can make your eyes water. Use middle-of-the-road vinegar for this, not your best 10-year-old stuff. In a pan, bring the vinegar to the boil. Leave it to simmer vigorously for 8–10 minutes, until it has reduced by about one-third and become quite syrupy. Watch the pan carefully towards the end, as you don't want it to go too far and burn. Leave the syrup to cool, then store in an airtight container. You can reduce a larger quantity of balsamic vinegar and use it in other dishes, as it will keep indefinitely.

29 Salmon and Mango Salsa

Informal supper

Preparation time 25 minutes

Serves 4 for lunch or
6 as a starter

**450 g (1 lb) salmon fillet,
skinned**

2 really ripe mangoes

**16 cherry tomatoes, halved,
or quartered if large**

**1/2 medium red onion, finely
diced**

**2 fresh green chilies, halved,
seeded and shredded or
chopped**

**4 tablespoons roughly chopped
fresh coriander**

juice of 1 lime

**freshly ground sea salt and
freshly ground black pepper**

This is a curious dish whose origin I've forgotten, but it is a lovely blend of fresh, zingy flavors. The salmon is added only partly cooked and becomes 'cured' by the acidity of the lime juice. The mango (which should be ripe) provides a sweet counterpoint, and the chili adds fire. Be generous with the coriander.

1 Heat a non-stick frying pan until quite hot, then add the salmon and cook for 2–3 minutes on each side until just cooked – it should still be pink in the middle. Lift out of the pan and cool.

2 Halve the mangoes by cutting down close to the flat pit on either side. Either peel off the skin using a potato peeler and dice the flesh into large chunks, or score through the flesh in a criss-cross pattern until almost touching the skin. Then push the flesh upwards and you will have a mango 'hedgehog,' or skin with chunks hanging on to it! Cut them free of the skin and put into a bowl.

3 Add the cherry tomatoes, red onion, chilies, coriander, a good squeeze of lime juice and salt and pepper.

4 Flake the salmon into large pieces and gently mix into the salsa, keeping it quite chunky. Divide into bowls and serve.

30 Seared Smoked Salmon, Crispy Beans and Chive Butter Sauce

Smart entertaining
Preparation time 20 minutes
Serves 4

oil, for deep-frying

350 g (12 oz) long beans, topped and strings removed

2 tablespoons chopped fresh chives

6 tablespoons Butter Sauce (see page 20)

250 g (9 oz) smoked salmon, sliced into escalopes (see page 10)

FOR THE BEER BATTER:

250 g (1³/₄ cups) self-raising flour

300 ml (1¹/₄ cups) lager

freshly ground sea salt and freshly ground black pepper

I've 'borrowed' this dish from my good friend and top chef Phil Vickery. He prepared something similar on a TV program called *Who'll Do the Pudding?* Tucking into the remains of Phil's food, I remarked that it was an excellent and clever dish. The ever-cynical Vickery replied that he was certain to find it in one of my books in the future, and sure enough here it is – my way, of course!

1 To make the batter, whisk the flour, lager and salt and pepper together until smooth.

2 Heat the oil to 190°C/375°F in an electric deep-fat fryer or large pan (use a cooking thermometer if necessary). Dip the beans into the batter a few at a time. Plunge into the hot oil and fry for a few minutes until crisp. Lift out and drain on paper towel. Keep warm in the oven with the door open while you fry the rest.

3 Stir the chives into the Butter Sauce and keep warm for a few minutes while you cook the salmon (but do not let it boil or it will split).

4 Heat a non-stick frying pan until very hot and fry the salmon escalopes on one side for 1 minute until beginning to brown but still moist. Lift out of the pan on to a plate and keep warm.

5 To serve, place a pile of beans on each plate and set a couple of slices of salmon on top, spoon over the chive butter sauce and serve immediately.

31 Char-grilled Salmon Steaks, Asparagus and Poached Egg

Informal supper
Preparation time 25 minutes
Serves 4

450 g (1 lb) fresh medium-sized asparagus spears

olive oil

2 tablespoons white wine vinegar or juice of 1 lemon

4 really fresh eggs, chilled

4 × 175 g (6 oz) salmon steaks or darnes (see pages 10–11)

extra virgin olive oil, to drizzle

freshly ground sea salt and freshly ground black pepper

50 g ($^1/_2$ cup) Parmesan cheese, freshly shaved

A simple but effective meeting of three ingredients which are happy inhabiting the same plate! If you can get them, duck's eggs are wonderfully rich, with gloriously deep orange yolks. Don't worry if you lose the odd bit of white during the poaching – it's the yolk you're after. Char-grilling the asparagus gives it a distinctive flavor which lifts the dish.

1 Preheat a grill pan until medium hot. Meanwhile, trim the ends off the asparagus spears. Using a potato peeler, shave the ends (if hard and woody) to a point. Toss the spears in a little olive oil to coat lightly. Grill for 5–7 minutes until tender and lightly charred. Keep warm.

2 Wipe the grill pan clean and heat up again while you poach the eggs. Pour 4 cm (1 $^1/_2$ inches) of boiling water and the vinegar or lemon juice into a clean frying pan or saucepan and place it over a low heat until there are a few bubbles on the base of the pan, but no more. Break the eggs carefully into the hot water and cook for 3–4 minutes, basting the tops of the eggs with a little of the hot water as they cook. Lift them out of the water with a slotted spoon and drain on kitchen paper.

3 Brush the salmon steaks with a little olive oil, then char-grill them (see page 12) and season.

4 Place a pile of asparagus on each of four warmed plates. Rest the salmon steaks alongside and top with a poached egg. Drizzle with olive oil and season with salt and pepper. Sprinkle with freshly shaved Parmesan and serve immediately.

32 Spicy Salmon Samosas with Chili Tomato Dip

Prepare in advance
Preparation time 25 minutes
Serves 6 as a starter

225 g (8 oz) salmon fillet, skinned

1 red onion, finely chopped

2 garlic cloves, finely chopped

a small knob of ginger, grated

1 fresh red chili, halved, seeded and chopped

50 g (2 oz) fresh coriander, stalks and all, chopped

olive oil

a dash of Thai fish sauce (*nam pla*)

a squeeze or two of lemon or lime juice

freshly ground sea salt and freshly ground black pepper

6 large sheets of filo pastry (Greek brands are best)

melted butter, for brushing

FOR THE CHILI TOMATO DIP:

4 tablespoons Heinz tomato ketchup

1 tablespoon rice wine vinegar

2 tablespoons sweet chili sauce (preferably Lingham's)

2 teaspoons dark soy sauce

The beauty of these samosas is that all the preparation is done in advance and you only have to put them in the oven at the last minute. Crunchy spicy pastry on the outside, soft scented salmon within – yum!

1 Preheat the oven to 220°C/425°F.

2 Cut the salmon into 2 cm (3/4 inch) cubes and place in a bowl. Mix in the onion, garlic, ginger, chili and coriander. Add a drop or two of olive oil, not too much Thai fish sauce as it's very strong, lemon or lime juice to taste, and a little salt and pepper.

3 Working quickly so the filo won't dry out, fold each sheet in half lengthways. Stack them up and keep under a *damp* (not wet) tea towel or plastic wrap.

4 Take one strip of filo, brush with a little melted butter and drop one-sixth of the filling on to the bottom short edge, about 3 cm (1 1/4 inches) from the end. Fold the end over the filling. Now pick up a bottom corner and fold diagonally over towards the long edge, to make a triangle. Keep folding until you come to the end. Brush with a little more melted butter and place on a baking sheet. Repeat with the other strips of filo.

5 Bake the samosas for 10–15 minutes until crisp and golden. While they are baking, mix the dipping sauce ingredients together and set aside. Brush the samosas with more melted butter and sprinkle with freshly ground sea salt as soon as they come out of the oven, and serve with the dipping sauce.

33 Smoked Salmon Eggs Benedict

Quick and easy
Preparation time 15 minutes
Serves 4

2 tablespoons white wine vinegar or juice of 1 lemon

4 large eggs

2 white English muffins, sliced in half

175 g (6 oz) sliced smoked salmon

250 ml (1 cup) Hollandaise Sauce (see page 21), or ready-made will do fine, warmed through

freshly ground sea salt and freshly ground black pepper

When experimenting with food, I often try replacing the ham or bacon in recipes with smoked salmon, with varying degrees of success. I think it's the similar intensity of the flavors that leads me to do this. One of the best dishes to emerge from my smoked salmon and ham 'gastrolab' was this.

1 Preheat the grill to the highest setting.

2 Poach the eggs as in the recipe for Char-grilled Salmon Steaks, Asparagus and Poached Egg (see page 50).

3 While the eggs are cooking, toast the muffin halves under the grill for a few seconds until lightly golden.

4 Place half a toasted muffin on each warmed serving plate and add a layer of smoked salmon. Gently place a poached egg on top and spoon over a generous helping of the Hollandaise Sauce. Season with the salt and pepper and serve.

34 Thai Salmon Cakes with Dipping Sauce

Hot and spicy
Preparation time 15 minutes, plus 1 hour chilling
Makes 12, serves 4 as a starter

600 g (1 lb 5 oz) salmon fillet, skinned

1 stem of lemon grass, outer leaves removed and finely chopped

50 g (2 oz) fresh coriander, stalks and all, roughly chopped

2 fresh green chilies, halved, seeded and chopped

finely grated rind of 1 lime

1 tablespoon Thai fish sauce (*nam pla*)

1 small egg

a little flour

vegetable oil, for frying

lemon wedges and coriander sprigs, to serve

FOR THE DIPPING SAUCE:

1 garlic clove, crushed

2 tablespoons Thai fish sauce (*nam pla*)

1 tablespoon fresh lime juice

1 teaspoon sugar

a few drops of home-made Chili Oil (see page 123) or ready-made chilli oil

1 tablespoon chopped fresh coriander

My globetrotting sister-in-law Liz and her partner Simon brought this recipe back from a cookery school they attended in Thailand. Whilst staying with me recently they offered to cook, and made the most awful mess of my beloved kitchen. They were instantly forgiven, however, when I tasted these astonishingly good fishcakes. Lemon grass can be very tough, so make sure you remove the outer leaves and chop very finely before blitzing in the food processor.

1 Cut away any brown bits of fat from the salmon and cut the flesh into cubes. Place in a food processor with the lemon grass, coriander, chilies, lime rind, Thai fish sauce and the egg. Blitz in short bursts until you get a smooth paste. Scrape out into a bowl, cover and chill for an hour.

2 Divide the mixture into 12, then roll into balls (wetting your hands will make this easier). Press each ball flat to form a cake, but don't make them too thin or they will be like rubber.

3 Mix all the dipping sauce ingredients together and set aside.

4 Dip each cake in the flour, shaking off the excess. Pour about 5 mm ($1/4$ inch) of oil into a frying pan and heat until a nut of salmon mixture will sizzle instantly. Now fry the cakes in batches for 1–2 minutes on each side until cooked and nicely brown. Drain on paper towel and serve with the dipping sauce, lemon wedges and coriander sprigs.

35 Smoked Salmon with a Boiled Egg and Capers

Quick and easy

Preparation time 8 minutes

Serves 4

4 medium free-range eggs

225 g (8 oz) sliced smoked salmon

juice of 1 lemon

4 teaspoons salted capers, rinsed and drained

freshly ground sea salt and freshly ground black pepper

This recipe was dreamt up when I was struck by the late night munchies. An examination of the fridge revealed smoked salmon and eggs. I was halfway to that old favorite, smoked salmon and scrambled eggs, when I discovered a jar of salted capers which was nearing its 'use-by' date – and so this dish was conceived and it was too good not to share with you.

1 To get the best results, the eggs should be at room temperature – this reduces the risk of them cracking when put into contact with the heat. Fill a small to medium pan three-quarters full with water and bring to the boil. Reduce the heat and allow to simmer. Carefully lower the eggs into the water and cook for approximately 5 minutes, depending on how you like them done (add or subtract 1 minute for hard or soft eggs respectively).

2 Lift the eggs from the water and pop under a cold tap for a few seconds: this stops the cooking process. Tap the eggs gently, cracking the shell all over, and remove the shell.

3 Place the salmon in a pile in the center of a plate and squeeze over a little lemon juice. Slice the eggs in half lengthways and place either side of the salmon. Sprinkle over a teaspoon of capers, season the eggs with salt and pepper, and the salmon with pepper only, and serve.

36 Salt-and-pepper Salmon with Szechuan Dipping Sauce

| Hot and spicy |
| Preparation time 25 minutes |
| Serves 4 as a starter, 2 as a main dish |

225 g (8 oz) salmon tail end fillet, skinned

1 1/2 teaspoons freshly ground sea salt

1 teaspoon Szechuan peppercorns

1 teaspoon black peppercorns

vegetable oil, for deep-frying

2 tablespoons self-raising flour

FOR THE SZECHUAN DIPPING SAUCE:

3 tablespoons light soy sauce

2 tablespoons rice wine or cider vinegar

1 teaspoon sweet chili sauce

3 teaspoons light sesame oil

2 green onions, finely chopped

freshly ground black pepper

Very simple, very tasty and very moreish. The key to success with this dish is to invest in an electric coffee grinder and use it to grind the salt-and-pepper mix. This does mean that your grinder can henceforth be used only for spices, but this is a good excuse to experiment with grinding all your own curry spices! Alternatively you can pound the mix in a pestle and mortar. Dry-frying salt and pepper together produces a really wonderful aromatic flavor that's more than just salt and pepper.

1 Cut the salmon into finger-sized strips, keeping a good thickness. Cover and chill.

2 Heat a dry, heavy-based frying pan over a medium heat. Add the salt and stir it around for a couple of minutes until it begins to look a bit gray. Tip it into a bowl, reheat the pan, then add the peppercorns and toss them around until they darken slightly and start to smell aromatic. Grind the salt and peppercorns to a fine powder in a coffee grinder or pestle and mortar.

3 Pour some oil into a large pan or electric deep-fat fryer so that it is about one-third full and heat it to 190°C/375°F (use a cooking thermometer if necessary). Mix the salt-and-pepper powder with the flour, place it in a plastic bag and add the salmon. Give the bag a good shake so that all the pieces of salmon become evenly coated in the highly seasoned flour.

4 Mix all the dipping sauce ingredients together in a small bowl and set aside.

5 Have a tray lined with paper towel handy. Tip the salmon fingers out of the bag on to a plate, then deep-fry 5–6 fingers at a time for just 30–45 seconds, until crisp and golden on the outside and still soft on the inside. Lift them out with a slotted spoon on to the kitchen paper to drain off the excess oil.

6 Pile the salt-and-pepper salmon on to four warmed plates and serve with the dipping sauce.

37 Smoked Salmon and Avocado Marie-Rose

Quick and easy
Preparation time 10 minutes
Serves 4

2 ripe avocados

a squeeze of lemon juice

200 g (7 oz) smoked salmon

freshly ground sea salt and freshly ground black pepper

1 Little Gem lettuce, shredded

lemon wedges, to serve

FOR THE MARIE-ROSE SAUCE:

5 tablespoons mayonnaise (preferably Hellmann's)

2 tablespoons tomato ketchup (preferably Heinz)

a pinch of cayenne pepper

I know that this dish sounds like a culinary cliché, but I have yet to meet a person who, deep down, doesn't love Marie-Rose sauce – that sublime blend of mayonnaise and tomato ketchup (it's got to be Hellmann's and Heinz, though; accept no substitutes). I've tried making the sauce using posh ingredients – a tomato fondue, crème fraîche, whipped cream – but I've never bettered the original. Add some ripe avocado (look for the ready-to-eat ones) and some smoked salmon, and you have a true rival to the prawn cocktail!

1 Halve the avocados, remove the pit, peel, cut into large chunks and toss with some lemon juice. Cut the smoked salmon into large pieces. Mix together in a bowl.

2 Make the Marie-Rose sauce by mixing together the mayonnaise, ketchup and a pinch of cayenne.

3 Add about 3 tablespoons of the sauce to the avocado/salmon mix and toss well. Taste, and add more sauce if necessary. Season with salt and pepper.

4 Divide the shredded lettuce between four glass dishes and place a pile of the salmon mix on top. Garnish with a lemon wedge or two.

38 Salmon and Goats' Cheese Tart with Tomato and Basil Salad

Informal supper
Preparation time 30 minutes, plus pastry chilling time
Serves 4–6

350 g (12 oz) salmon fillet, skinned

50 ml (¼ cup) milk

225 g (8 oz) smoked salmon pieces

2 eggs

2 egg yolks

200 ml (7 fl oz) crème fraîche

1 tablespoon chopped fresh tarragon

freshly ground sea salt and freshly ground black pepper

175 g (6 oz) goats' cheese, crumbled

thinly sliced tomato and shredded basil leaves, dressed, to serve

FOR THE PASTRY:

225 g (1 ½ cups) all-purpose flour

½ teaspoon salt

115 g (½ cup) butter, chilled

2 egg yolks

1–2 tablespoons chilled water

There is something very satisfying about learning to make your own pastry, and it's much easier than some would suggest. A food processor speeds up the job, but it's not quite as satisfying as using your fingers. If you're stuck for time the quality of ready-made pre-rolled pastry is now very good, so there's no excuse for not giving this a go. A loose-bottomed tart tin is a useful and inexpensive investment, and they seem to become more non-stick with use.

1 To make the pastry, put the flour, salt and butter in a food processor and blitz until it looks like fine breadcrumbs. Add the egg yolks mixed with the water and whizz in short bursts until it just starts coming together. Tip out on to a floured board and knead gently until smooth. Cover in plastic wrap and rest in the fridge for 30 minutes.

2 Meanwhile, put the salmon fillet in a small pan and pour over the milk. Bring this to just under boiling point, then cover with a lid and steam or simmer for 2 minutes until almost cooked through. Leave to cool.

3 Roll out the pastry on a floured surface and use to line a 20 cm (8 inch) × 3 cm (1¼ inch) deep tart tin or four deep 10 cm (4 inch) tart tins. Prick the bases with a fork and either freeze or chill for 15 minutes. Then line with baking parchment, fill with baking beans or dried beans, place on a baking sheet and bake in the oven at 190°C/375°F for 15 minutes (10 minutes for the tartlets) to set the pastry. Remove the paper and beans and bake for a further 10 minutes, then take out and leave to cool slightly on the baking sheet.

4 Lift the salmon out of the milk, break into large flakes and scatter over the base of the tart. Scatter the smoked salmon pieces on top.

5 Beat the eggs and yolks into the poaching milk with the crème fraîche. Stir in the tarragon and season well (but not too much salt). Pour all over the salmon, give the tart tin a bit of a shake to settle the liquid, then scatter the crumbled goats' cheese on top.

6 Return the tart to the oven and bake for 30–35 minutes, until just set and golden brown on top. The tartlets will take about 20 minutes. Serve the tart warm, not hot, with the tomato and basil salad.

39 Salmon Mousseline with Butter Sauce

Smart entertaining
Preparation time 45 minutes, plus chilling time
Serves 6

450 g (1 lb) salmon fillet, skinned

1 medium egg

450 ml (1 3/4 cups) 35% cream

freshly ground sea salt and freshly ground black pepper

a pinch of cayenne pepper

1 tablespoon lemon juice

1 quantity Butter Sauce (see page 20), warmed through

Avruga or Keta caviar and chopped fresh parsley, to serve

Mousseline is quite an old-fashioned dish, but when done right its melt-in-the-mouth sensation is fantastic. Raw mousseline mixture can't stand the heat, so try to keep everything as cool as possible during preparation. I always put the bowl and blade from the food processor into the freezer for an hour before starting as this helps to counteract the friction heat caused by the whizzing of the blades.

1 If serving immediately, preheat the oven to 190°C/375°F.

2 Break down the salmon in a food processor for 1–2 minutes. When it's smooth and thick (you may have to scrape down the sides a couple of times), add the egg and whizz the mixture for another 1–2 minutes.

3 Scrape the fish out into a fine-mesh stainless steel sieve and force it through (this prevents any sinew getting into the mix). I usually wear a rubber glove, which makes it easier to force the fish through. Transfer the salmon to a shallow metal bowl and refrigerate for an hour.

4 Remove the bowl from the fridge and place it into another bowl (of similar size, or slightly wider), half filled with ice (this keeps the temperature of the fish low and helps prevent the mousseline from splitting).

5 Gradually start working in the cream a little at a time with a wooden spoon. The consistency should be as soft as possible, but still keeping its shape in the bowl. At this point, add a little more cream and season with salt directly on to the cream. This prevents the salt making direct contact with the fish, which would lead to graininess in the mousse. Add the cayenne pepper and lemon juice, then check the seasoning and consistency. It should taste fresh and quite salty and lemony – the cooking process will draw in the seasoning – while the texture should again be smooth, but still holding its shape.

6 Butter six dariole molds or ramekins. Divide the mousseline between the molds, filling to within 1 cm (1/2 inch) of the top, firmly tapping each on the worktop to release any trapped air. If not cooking immediately, cover each filled mold with plastic wrap and refrigerate until ready to cook. They will keep for a maximum of 8 hours.

7 When ready to cook, cover the top of each mold with a little square of grease-proof paper or wrapping from the butter pack. Place the molds into a roasting pan and pour in enough boiling water to come halfway up the sides of the molds. Place the pan into the preheated oven and cook for about 12 minutes until very slightly raised on top.

8 Tip each mold on to a warmed plate, spoon over some of the Butter Sauce, then top with a generous dollop of Avruga and a sprinkling of parsley.

40 Salmon Crumble with Lemon Zucchini

Prepare in advance
Preparation time 25 minutes
Serves 4

Butter, for greasing

4 × 140 g (5 oz) salmon fillets

FOR THE CRUMBLE TOPPING:

85 g (1 cup) fresh breadcrumbs

25 g (¹/4 cup) Parmesan cheese, freshly grated

2 tablespoons chopped fresh mixed herbs (parsley and basil)

2 tablespoons melted butter

freshly ground sea salt and freshly ground black pepper

FOR THE LEMON ZUCCHINI:

3 tablespoons olive oil

1 garlic clove, crushed

2 medium zucchini, thinly sliced

juice of ¹/2 lemon

This dish can work equally well as a light lunch or as a dinner party main course. The great thing about the crumble topping is that you can prepare it in advance, sprinkle it on top of the salmon and keep the whole lot in the fridge until you're ready to put it in the oven. Once you've mastered the technique, you can experiment with different-flavored crumbles. Herbs, garlic, chili and spices all work well. Whichever flavor you use, you'll always have that fantastic contrast between the crunchy, crumbly topping and the soft, moist salmon.

1 Preheat the oven to 220°C/425°F. Grease a baking pan with butter and lay the salmon fillets inside.

2 Put all the crumble ingredients into a bowl and lightly rub together until large lumps begin to form. Sprinkle evenly over the fillets and bake in the oven for 8–10 minutes until crisp and golden. If they are not golden enough after this time, finish off under the grill – you don't want the salmon to overcook.

3 Meanwhile, make the lemon zucchini. Heat the oil in a frying pan, add the garlic and cook for 30 seconds. Throw in the zucchini and stir-fry for 3 minutes until beginning to color and soften. Squeeze in the lemon juice and add salt and pepper to taste.

4 Serve the salmon crumble with a portion of lemon zucchini on the side.

41 Toasted Bagel, Scrambled Eggs and Smoked Salmon

Quick and easy
Preparation time 5 minutes
Serves 2

4 eggs

10 g (1 tablespoon) lightly salted butter

1 plain bagel, sliced in half

40 g (1 1/2 oz) smoked salmon

10 g (1/2 oz) chives, chopped, to serve

Scrambled eggs and smoked salmon go together like ham and eggs or fish and chips – natural partners in the food world. To make this dish sing you must ensure that the scrambled eggs aren't overcooked (always remember that the eggs continue to cook when removed from the stove), so have the bagels and smoked salmon ready. I much prefer my smoked salmon raw and draped over the eggs; I find cooking it in the egg mix robs it of its texture. Of course, you could serve this on toast, but there's something about the unique chewy taste of bagels that complements the soft eggs and silky smoked salmon.

1 Beat the eggs in a bowl. Melt the butter in a heavy frying pan over a low heat. Add the eggs and cook on a low heat for 2–3 minutes, stirring and scraping the pan continuously.

2 Meanwhile, toast the bagel halves until golden brown. Place them on serving plates.

3 Once the eggs have reached a luscious, creamy consistency, remove them from the heat and divide between the bagel halves.

4 Top with the smoked salmon, scrunching the slices slightly to create a little height. Sprinkle with the chopped chives and serve.

42 Smoked Salmon Pâté with Classic Melba Toast

Prepare in advance
Preparation time 10 minutes
Serves 4–6

115 g (¹/₂ cup) unsalted butter, cubed and softened

115 g (¹/₂ cup) cream cheese (preferably Philadelphia), softened

400 g (14 oz) smoked salmon, finely shredded

juice of 1 lemon

freshly ground sea salt and freshly ground black pepper

8–12 slices of white bread

This recipe is a classic. You can add grated lemon rind, a bit of mustard, anchovy essence, chopped parsley, chopped dill, chopped capers – whatever takes your fancy. I have it on good authority that this used to be served in the scooped out shells of lemons – life is just too short for lemon scooping, but tasting this again makes me wonder why the recipe was ever forgotten!

1 Put all the ingredients, except for the bread, in a food processor. Blitz until smooth, scraping down the sides a couple of times. If making by hand, beat the butter and cream cheese together in a bowl, tip in the salmon and beat well to mix. Add as much lemon juice as you like to balance the richness of the butter and cream cheese, and season well with salt and pepper.

2 Cover and allow the flavors to develop in a cool place for a couple of hours. Whatever you do, don't serve this straight from the fridge – it won't spread and it will have lost its taste, as most things do when served very cold.

3 Preheat the grill. Pop the bread into a toaster and lightly toast on both sides. As soon as it comes out of the toaster, cut off the crusts with a serrated knife and cut in half horizontally to give two thin slices of bread toasted on one side only.

4 Place on a baking sheet, untoasted side up, and grill for a few seconds until nicely colored and crispy. (Watch them like a hawk – they burn very easily.) Repeat until all the remaining bread has been toasted in this way.

5 Pile the pâté into a large bowl and pass round the Melba toast for everyone to help themselves to a dollop of pâté and a couple of pieces of toast.

43 Salmon Teriyaki Sticks

Low fat
Preparation time 15 minutes, plus soaking time
Serves 4

450 g (1 lb) salmon fillet

FOR THE TERIYAKI MARINADE:

1 teaspoon superfine granulated sugar

1 tablespoon mirin (Japanese rice wine for cooking) or dry sherry

2 tablespoons light soy sauce (preferably Kikkoman's)

1 tablespoon sunflower oil

1 teaspoon Dijon mustard

a squeeze of lime juice

2 tablespoons runny honey, warmed

I'm very partial to salmon teriyaki, but always found it a bit tricky to cook. This was because I'd previously cooked it in a frying pan, where it tended to stick as the honey in the marinade burned before the salmon was cooked. A flash of inspiration led me to try leaving the honey out of the marinade, reserving it to brush over the salmon once it was cooked, and – bingo! – trouble-free teriyaki ever since. Remember: soaking the wooden skewers in water before grilling will prevent them from burning and disintegrating.

1 Soak eight bamboo skewers in cold water for at least 30 minutes.

2 Cut the salmon into long, thin strips, 2.5 cm (1 inch) wide and about 5 mm (1/4 inch) thick.

3 Mix all the marinade ingredients together, except for the honey, and toss the salmon strips in it. Cover and leave for 10 minutes to marinate. Heat a grill pan (or grill).

4 Thread the salmon on to the skewers in a zigzag fashion. Brush the kebabs with a little extra oil and grill for 1–2 minutes on each side. Lift them off the grill as they are done and brush them with warm honey before serving.

44 Salmon Satay

450 g (1 lb) salmon fillet

FOR THE MARINADE:

3 garlic cloves, finely chopped

1 teaspoon ground coriander

1 teaspoon ground cumin

2 tablespoons soft brown sugar

2 tablespoons Thai fish sauce

6 tablespoons Tamarind Water (see below)

2 tablespoons peanut oil

FOR THE SATAY SAUCE:

200 ml (3/4 cup) peanut oil

85 g (3/4 cup) raw peanuts

2 fresh green chilies

1 cm (1/2 inch) piece fresh ginger, peeled

3 garlic cloves, peeled

200 ml (3/4 cup) coconut milk

2 teaspoons dark soy sauce

4 teaspoons Thai fish sauce

1 teaspoon soft brown sugar

juice of 1/2 lime

freshly ground sea salt and freshly ground black pepper

3 tablespoons chopped fresh coriander

Being a country boy, I was brought up on a diet of roasts, stews and plain vegetables. It wasn't until I joined the Navy and traveled the world that I experienced the wonders of herbs and spices. The first spicy dish I ever ate was chicken satay sticks cooked over a barbecue on the waterfront in Singapore. The memory of that flavor stays with me today, so it was logical for me to develop a recipe for salmon satay.

Don't be put off by the lengthy list of ingredients. The sauce and marinade are both easy to make and very addictive, so you'll use up any specially bought ingredients. Don't over-process the sauce; it should have a rustic feel to it. If you want to be really authentic, double the amount of chilies, but do warn your guests.

1 Soak eight bamboo skewers in cold water for at least 30 minutes.

2 Cut the salmon into long, thin strips, 2.5 cm (1 inch) wide and about 5 mm (1/4 inch) thick. Thread the salmon on to the skewers in a zigzag fashion and lay them in a shallow dish.

3 Mix the marinade ingredients together and pour over the salmon sticks. Turn around in the marinade to coat. Cover and leave for an hour, turning occasionally.

4 Meanwhile, make the satay sauce. Heat the oil in a medium pan until very hot, then add the peanuts and stir gently until golden. Quickly tip them into a sieve placed over a bowl, then put them in a blender with half the reserved oil and all the remaining sauce ingredients, except the coriander. Whizz until smooth. Stir in the remaining oil and the coriander and pour into a bowl.

5 Heat a grill pan (or grill). Remove the salmon sticks from the marinade, brush with a little extra oil and grill for 1 minute on each side. Lift them off the grill as they are done and serve them in a pile with the satay dipping sauce.

Tamarind Water

To make tamarind water, soak about 50 g (2 oz) dried tamarind pulp in 8 tablespoons warm water for 10 minutes. Work the fibrous pulp with your fingers to break it up, then press through a sieve to extract the liquid.

45 Salmon Sashimi

Low fat
Preparation time 10-15minutes
Serves 4

450 g (1 lb) very fresh salmon fillet, skinned

3 teaspoons wasabi paste (I prefer the dried sachet variety)

25 g (1 oz) Japanese pickled ginger

4 tablespoons soy sauce (preferably Kikkoman's)

2 tablespoons Japanese pickled ginger juice

As sashimi is simply raw fish, served with wasabi (wickedly hot Japanese horseradish), pickled ginger and soy sauce, it goes without saying that the fish must be top quality and, of course, really fresh. Salmon makes particularly good sashimi due to its oily texture, and you will be amazed at how tasty raw fish can be. A common misconception is that the fish should be sliced paper thin; in fact it should be around 5 mm (1/4 inch) thick and cut at a slight angle. Do give this a try, especially if you can find organic Orkney salmon – you won't be disappointed.

1 Cut the salmon in half lengthways along the natural line that separates the top of the salmon from the thinner belly. Take each half and slice into 5 mm (1/4 inch) slices. Lift the slices as cut with a palette knife and slide on to the serving plate; the fish should look as natural as possible.

2 If necessary, make the wasabi according to the sachet instructions. Place a little pile on the serving plate beside the salmon.

3 Finely shred the pickled ginger and arrange in a small pile on the serving plate next to the salmon and wasabi.

4 Finally, mix the soy sauce with the pickled ginger juice and pour it into a small dipping saucer, place on the serving plate and serve with chopsticks.

46 Smoked Salmon and Herb Ravioli with Chive Butter Sauce

Smart entertaining
Preparation time 45 minutes, plus chilling time
Serves 4 as a starter, 2 as a main dish

FOR THE SMOKED SALMON AND HERB MOUSSELINE:

115 g (4 oz) smoked salmon, diced

freshly ground sea salt and freshly ground black pepper

a squeeze of lemon juice

1 egg white, chilled

2 tablespoons finely chopped parsley and chives

50 g (2 oz) salmon fillet, skinned and finely diced

125 ml (1/2 cup) 35% cream, chilled

FOR THE FRESH PASTA DOUGH:

140 g (5 oz) all-purpose flour or Italian '00' flour

1 medium egg

1 medium egg yolk

FOR THE CHIVE BUTTER SAUCE:

1 quantity Butter Sauce (see page 20), warmed through

1 tablespoon finely chopped chives

This isn't the easiest recipe in the world, but most of the work can be done in advance, and if you get it right you'll be rewarded not only with a sublime dish but also with the knowledge that you've mastered two valuable skills: making fresh pasta and fish mousse. The secret of perfect pasta lies in getting the dough to just the right consistency – too much flour and it'll be dry and crack when you roll it out; too little and the dough will be soft and stick to itself. The perfect dough should have the consistency of plasticine and shouldn't need to be dredged in flour to stop it sticking.

Having produced a good dough, you need to work it really well to get a smooth, silky texture. I find the best way to do this is to pass the dough through a pasta roller on its widest setting at least 12 times, folding it in half between each pass.

1 Season the diced smoked salmon with salt and pepper and add the lemon juice. Cover and chill.

2 To make the pasta dough, place the flour in a food processor and start giving it a whizz round. Add the whole egg and egg yolk and keep whizzing until the mixture resembles fine breadcrumbs (it shouldn't be dusty, nor should it be a big, gooey ball). This takes 2–3 minutes.

3 Tip out the dough and knead it briskly for 1 minute to form a ball shape – it should be quite stiff and hard to knead. Cover with plastic wrap and leave to rest in a cool place for at least 1 hour before using.

4 Meanwhile, make the mousseline. Break down the smoked salmon in a food processor for 1–2 minutes. When it's smooth and thick (you may have to scrape down the sides a couple of times), add the egg white and whizz the mixture for another 1–2 minutes.

5 Scrape the fish out into a fine-mesh stainless steel sieve and force it through (this prevents any sinew getting into the mix). I usually wear a rubber glove, which makes it easier to force the fish through. Transfer the salmon to a shallow metal bowl, beat in the herbs and diced fresh salmon and cover and chill for at least an hour.

6 Remove from the fridge and gradually start working in the cream, a little at a time, with a wooden spoon. You want the consistency of the mixture to be as soft as possible, but still keeping its shape in the bowl. Season the last bit of cream with a little salt and quickly fold in to the mix. This prevents the salt making direct contact with the fish, which would give the mousse a grainy texture.

7 Now unwrap the pasta dough and cut into two pieces. Flatten each piece with a rolling pin to about 5 mm (1/4 inch) thickness. Fold over the dough and pass it through the pasta machine at its widest setting, refolding and rolling 12 times (not changing the setting) until you have a rectangular shape 7.5 × 18 cm (3 × 7 inches). It's important to work the dough until it is nice and shiny, as this gives it the *al dente* texture. Repeat with the second piece of dough.

8 Now you are ready to roll out. Start with the pasta machine at its widest setting and pass each piece of dough through the rollers. Do not fold but repeat this process, decreasing the roller setting down grade by grade with each pass, taking it down to its lowest setting. This may seem thin, but remember that you will have a double layer of the pasta when the ravioli is folded. Use straight away to make the ravioli.

9 Lay the two lengths of pasta on a *very* lightly floured work surface. Place scant teaspoons of mousseline in mounds slightly left of center along the length of each piece of pasta. Make sure they are well spaced. Dampen the long edges and in between each mound with a little water on a pastry brush. Flip the free length of the pasta over the filling and press in between each mound to exclude all air and seal *before* sealing the long edge. Trim the long edge with a pastry wheel, then cut into ravioli. Lay these in a single layer on a dry tea towel until ready to cook.

10 Add the chives to the Butter Sauce and set aside while you cook the pasta. Drop the pasta into a large pot of boiling, salted water, stirring until it comes back to the boil again. Cook for 2 1/2 minutes, then remove the ravioli with a slotted spoon and serve immediately with the chive butter sauce.

WORDS OF WARNING

Always cover sitting dough with plastic wrap or a damp tea towel to prevent it drying out.

Do not add oil to the cooking water. It is a fallacy that it prevents sticking and is therefore a complete waste of oil.

Do not dredge the pasta in flour to prevent sticking, as the flour turns to glue when cooked and, ironically, causes the pasta to stick together. (Using fine Italian '00' flour will help – this is the finest grade of soft wheat flour available.)

47 Strozzapreti, Smoked Salmon and Parmesan Cream

Quick and easy

Preparation time 20 minutes

Serves 6

450 g (1 lb) dried strozzapreti (or other similar pasta shape)

freshly ground sea salt and freshly ground black pepper

225 g (8 oz) sliced smoked salmon

16 cherry tomatoes, halved

4 tablespoons chopped fresh parsley

300 ml (1 1/4 cups) 35% cream

6 tablespoons grated Parmesan cheese

Strozzapreti, which, in typically quaint Italian parlance, means 'priest stranglers,' are short and twisted pasta shapes. They're really good at picking up lots of sauce, which is exactly what's needed for this delicious and rich blend of Parmesan and heavy cream. This dish is really quick and easy to prepare; the only downside is those pesky calories. As with all simple dishes the quality of the raw materials is of paramount importance, so do try to get Reggiano Parmesan – it's by far the best, and you can always tell if it's genuine as it has the word *Reggiano* stamped all over the rind.

1 Cook the pasta according to the packet instructions, in a huge pan of boiling salted water – the bigger the pan, the less chance of sticking. Give it a stir occasionally.

2 Cut the smoked salmon into long strips and mix with the cherry tomatoes and half the parsley.

3 Pour the cream into a pan and bring to the boil, then boil for 1 minute until it starts to thicken, stir in 4 tablespoons of the Parmesan cheese and season with black pepper.

4 Drain the pasta and toss with the Parmesan cream. Either serve the pasta with the smoked salmon mixture piled on top, or toss the whole lot together and serve immediately, sprinkled with the remaining Parmesan and parsley.

48 Poached Salmon, Pappardelle, Rocket and Parmesan Pesto

Quick and easy
Preparation time 15 minutes
Serves 4

450 g (1 lb) salmon fillet, skinned

350 g (12 oz) dried pappardelle

2 tablespoons olive oil

4 tablespoons home-made Pesto (see page 13) or ready-made pesto

115 g (4 oz) rocket leaves, washed and dried

freshly ground sea salt and freshly ground black pepper

50 g (¹/₂ cup) Parmesan cheese shavings

This is exactly the sort of dish that I like to eat on a summer evening. If you've made the pesto in advance, cooking the final dish is easy; the rocket should just be wilted through the pasta rather than cooked, so that it keeps its color and texture. It is perfect served with a tomato and basil salad and a big bottle of Aussie Chardonnay.

1 Lay the salmon in a shallow pan and pour in enough water to cover. Slowly bring up to just below boiling point, then simmer gently for 5 minutes until the salmon is just cooked. Lift out of the water on to a plate and allow to cool slightly before pulling into large flakes.

2 Put the pappardelle into a very large pan of boiling salted water and cook according to the packet instructions until *al dente*. Drain well, return to the hot, dry pan and immediately toss with the olive oil and pesto. Add the rocket and stir into the pappardelle until it begins to wilt.

3 Fold through the salmon and divide between four warmed plates. Season with salt and pepper and scatter with Parmesan shavings.

49 Grilled Salmon with Roasted Vegetable Penne

Informal supper
Preparation time 35 minutes
Serves 4

1 small eggplant, cut into 1 cm (1/2 inch) slices lengthways, salted and drained

2 long red peppers, halved and seeded

2 medium zucchini, sliced lengthways into three

100 ml (6 tablespoons) olive oil, plus extra for brushing

350 g (12 oz) dried penne

4 tablespoons roughly chopped fresh basil

2 tablespoons pine nuts, toasted

juice of 1/2 lemon

freshly ground sea salt and freshly ground black pepper

4 × 140 g (5 oz) salmon fillets

50 g (1/2 cup) Parmesan cheese, grated

You really need a ridged grill pan or a barbecue to give the vegetables the correct charred flavor. Alternatively, you can roast them in the top of a very hot oven, but I do miss that slightly bitter smoky edge you get from char-grilling. The vegetables can be roasted in advance and reheated when needed. In fact, they keep for up to a week in the fridge, stored in a jar under a layer of olive oil.

1 Heat a ridged grill pan until very hot. Rinse the eggplant well and then pat dry. Brush the vegetables with olive oil and cook on the grill pan until well colored and tender, then place in a bowl to cool slightly.

2 Cook the pasta according to the packet instructions until *al dente*. Meanwhile, dice the char-grilled vegetables into 1 cm (1/2 inch) chunks.

3 When the pasta's ready, drain and return to the hot pan, then add the olive oil, diced vegetables, basil, pine nuts, lemon juice, freshly ground sea salt and freshly ground black pepper. Keep warm while you cook the salmon.

4 Reheat the griddle pan. Brush the salmon fillets with a little oil and place on the pan. After 2 minutes, turn through 90 degrees, cook for another 2 minutes, then turn over and repeat. There should be nicely criss-crossed grill marks on the salmon. Add the Parmesan to the pasta. Divide the roasted vegetable penne between four serving bowls, place a salmon fillet on top of each and serve.

Smoked Salmon 'Carbonara'

Quick and easy
Preparation time 15 minutes
Serves 4

225 g (8 oz) sliced smoked salmon

350 g (12 oz) fresh or dried linguine or spaghetti

25 g (2 tablespoons) butter

2 garlic cloves, lightly crushed, but still whole

4 tablespoons dry white wine

3 fresh eggs

85 g (³/₄ cup) Parmesan cheese, grated

3 tablespoons chopped fresh parsley

freshly ground sea salt and freshly ground black pepper

The sauce for this carbonara is just whole whisked-up eggs folded through the hot linguine to make a creamy scrambled egg, which clings to the pasta. The secret, as with scrambled eggs, is not to overcook, and there's usually enough residual heat in the pan to cook the eggs off the stove. The smoked salmon replaces the pancetta used in the original recipe. Personally, I don't like the smoked salmon to be cooked all the way through, and usually just scatter it over before serving.

1 Cut the smoked salmon into long strips and set aside.

2 Cook the linguine according to the packet instructions in boiling salted water until *al dente*.

3 While the linguine is cooking, melt the butter in a medium saucepan and add the garlic. Cook the garlic until golden, then lift out it and throw it away. Splash in the wine and boil until it has almost disappeared. Cool slightly, then beat in the eggs, Parmesan, parsley, salt and pepper.

4 Drain the linguine and return to the hot pan. Quickly pour in the egg mixture and toss well. The residual heat should start to cook the eggs – if not, stir over a very gentle heat for a second or two to cook a bit more.

5 Pile into four warmed bowls and scatter the smoked salmon on top. Serve immediately.

51 Lemon Butter Baked Salmon, Tagliatelle and Parsley

Quick and easy
Preparation time 25 minutes
Serves 4

50 g (¹/₄ cup) butter

finely grated rind and juice of 1 lemon

freshly ground sea salt and freshly ground black pepper

4 × 175 g (6 oz) salmon fillets, skinned

350 g (12 oz) dried tagliatelle

4 tablespoons chopped fresh parsley

This dish is so simple yet so tasty. If you've got time, you could use home-made pasta here; if not, dried thin tagliatelle or linguine will do a fabulous job. What make this dish taste so good are the salmon juices, which mingle with the butter and lemon in the oven, so when you're pouring them over the pasta, use a spatula to scrape out every last drop.

1 Preheat the oven to 200°C/400°F.

2 Melt the butter in a small roasting pan and add the lemon rind and juice. Season with plenty of salt and pepper.

3 Lay the salmon fillets in the roasting pan and turn them around in the lemony butter, ending up skinned-side down. Place into the oven for 7–8 minutes until cooked through but still moist inside. To test whether the salmon is done, give the fattest part a gentle squeeze and it should give slightly – if it's still wobbly, pop it back into the oven for another couple of minutes. If it feels solid, it's overcooked.

4 Meanwhile, throw the pasta into a large pan of boiling salted water and cook according to the packet instructions until *al dente*. Take the salmon out of the roasting pan and place on a warmed plate. Drain the pasta, mix with the lemony buttery juices collected in the salmon roasting pan and add the parsley. Divide the pasta between four warmed plates. Set a baked salmon fillet on top and tuck in!

52 Tagliatelle with Seared Salmon and Roast Tomato Sauce

Informal supper
Preparation time 25 minutes
Serves 4

450 g (1 lb) midi plum tomatoes, halved lengthways

5 tablespoons olive oil

1 garlic clove, crushed

freshly ground sea salt and freshly ground black pepper

350 g (12 oz) dried egg tagliatelle (look out for the De Cecco brand)

4 tablespoons roughly chopped fresh basil

225 g (8 oz) young spinach, washed and picked

4 × 115 g (4 oz) salmon fillets

The roast tomato sauce is a rustic Mediterranean sauce that is cooked in the oven and has a nice, chunky texture. However, you do need good tomatoes to get the correct sweet flavor. I usually use small vine tomatoes or baby plum tomatoes. As the spinach is just being wilted through the pasta, it's best to use baby spinach leaves.

1 Preheat the oven to 200°C/400°F. Place the plum tomatoes in a roasting pan, drizzle over about 3 tablespoons of the olive oil, add the garlic and season with freshly ground sea salt and freshly ground black pepper. Put them in the oven and roast for 15–20 minutes, until the tomatoes are just starting to slump or split.

2 Cook the pasta according to the packet instructions until *al dente*, drain and return to the pan.

3 Remove the pan of tomatoes from the oven and, using the back of a fork, mash them down. Add the basil and stir through. Check the seasoning and tip into the pan of pasta. Then add the spinach, mix well and keep warm.

4 Heat a non-stick frying pan until very hot, then add the salmon fillets. Sear on one side only, removing when the top side just starts to change color.

5 To serve, divide the pasta between four warmed bowls (a pasta-lifter is a very useful thing to have here) and place the seared salmon fillets on top.

53 Salmon Laksa

Hot and spicy
Preparation time 25 minutes
Serves 4

2 fresh red chilies (more if you like)

2 garlic cloves, crushed

5 cm (2 inch) piece fresh ginger, peeled and crushed

1 teaspoon ground coriander

4 tablespoons roughly chopped fresh coriander

2 tablespoons roughly chopped fresh mint

1 tablespoon light sesame oil

1 tablespoon sunflower oil

2 × 400 ml (14 fl oz) cans coconut milk

600 ml (2 1/2 cups) fish or vegetable stock

3 tablespoons Thai fish sauce (*nam pla*)

juice of 1 lemon

3 green onions, finely sliced

350 g (12 oz) salmon fillet, cut into medallions (see pages 10–11)

140 g (5 oz) dried flat rice noodles

Along with satay, laksas were my first introduction to spicy foods, enjoyed from the street stalls of Singapore when I was a Naval cadet. At the time I was mystified as to where these incredible flavors came from – the ingredients seemed impossibly exotic in the late 1970s. Now, of course, they are available in every large supermarket, and it's possible to recreate the smells and flavors of Singapore in your own home.

1 Put the chilies, garlic, ginger, ground coriander, fresh coriander, mint and sesame oil into a food processor and blitz to a coarse paste.

2 Heat a large pan, add the sunflower oil, then the paste and fry for 1 minute, stirring well. Add the coconut milk and stock, bring to the boil and simmer for 10 minutes. Add the fish sauce, lemon juice, green onions and salmon. Stir gently for a few seconds.

3 Meanwhile, cook the noodles according to the packet instructions.

4 Warm four bowls, divide the noodles between them and ladle on the soup, ensuring the salmon is equally divided between the bowls.

54 Seared Salmon with Noodles and Chili Vegetables

Hot and spicy
Preparation time 30 minutes
Serves 4

225 g (8 oz) medium egg noodles

juice of 1 lemon

3 tablespoons roughly chopped fresh coriander

4 teaspoons light sesame oil

4 × 175 g (6 oz) skinless salmon fillets

freshly ground sea salt and freshly ground black pepper

FOR THE CHILI VEGETABLES:

1 small cauliflower, cut into small florets

1/2 Chinese cabbage, shredded

6 green onions, cut into 3 cm (1 1/4 inch) lengths

2 tablespoons vegetable oil

1 red pepper, seeded and sliced into 5 mm (1/4 inch) strips

2 fresh red or green chilies, seeded and sliced into rings

2 garlic cloves, finely chopped

4 cm (1 1/2 inch) piece fresh ginger, peeled, finely sliced and cut into shreds

1 tablespoon dark soy sauce

2 tablespoons Thai fish sauce (*nam pla*)

2 tablespoons kechap manis (sweet Indonesian soy sauce)

This combination of Oriental flavors will transform any vegetables loitering at the back of your fridge. Cauliflower works so well here, soaking up all the cooking juices. If you can't get kechap manis, you could use a tablespoon of dark brown sugar mixed with a tablespoon of dark soy sauce instead. I owe a credit to Paul Rankin – the chili vegetables were his idea!

1 To make the chili vegetables, cook the cauliflower in salted boiling water for about 4 minutes until *al dente*, adding the cabbage to the pan for the last 15 seconds. Drain well and refresh in plenty of cold water. Drain again and place in a bowl with the green onions.

2 Next, cook the noodles. Bring a large pan of water to the boil, add a teaspoon of salt and drop in the noodles. Remove the pan from the heat and stir with a fork. Leave to stand for 4 minutes, stir again, then drain in a colander. Return the noodles to the warm pan, squeeze over half the lemon juice, sprinkle over the coriander and fold through. Cover and keep warm.

3 Heat the vegetable oil in a large frying pan or wok. Add the red pepper, chilies, garlic and ginger and sauté over a high heat for 30 seconds. Add the cauliflower, cabbage and green onions and cook for a further 2 minutes until thoroughly heated through. Add the soy sauce, Thai fish sauce and kechap manis and about 2 tablespoons water. Continue to cook for another 30 seconds, or until the juices thicken slightly.

4 Heat the sesame oil in a medium frying pan. Once hot, add the salmon fillets and pan-fry until cooked through and nicely colored. Sprinkle over the remaining lemon juice and season.

5 Divide the noodles between four warmed serving plates. Place a salmon fillet on each and spoon over the chili vegetables.

55 Steamed Salmon with Spicy Noodles

Quick and easy
Preparation 15 minutes
Serves 4

1 tablespoon sunflower oil

4 × 140 g (5 oz) salmon fillets, skinned

1 fresh red chili, finely diced

1/2 red pepper, very finely sliced

3 green onions, finely chopped

1 garlic clove, finely chopped

2.5 cm (1 inch) piece ginger, peeled and finely chopped

1 tablespoon Thai fish sauce (*nam pla*)

1 tablespoon lime juice

freshly ground sea salt and freshly ground black pepper

1 vegetable stock cube

200 g (7 oz) medium egg noodles

2 tablespoons roughly chopped fresh coriander

This dish is really just an upmarket Pot Noodle, although instead of being full of chemicals and 'E' numbers it's full of fresh-tasting, zingy, spicy ingredients. Egg noodles are one of the great storecupboard standbys and take only 4 minutes, soaking in boiling water to prepare.

1 To steam the salmon, fill the base of a steamer with hot water and place over the heat. Put a little oil on the base of a large heatproof plate that fits inside your steamer. Lay the salmon on top and scatter over the chili, red pepper, green onions, garlic, ginger, Thai fish sauce, lime juice and seasoning. Cover with plastic wrap. Lay a clean J-cloth in the steamer to help lift out the plate when cooked, and set the plate of salmon on top. Cover and steam for about 8 minutes.

2 Meanwhile, cook the noodles. Bring a large pan of water to the boil. Add the stock cube and a pinch of salt, stir until dissolved, then drop in the noodles. Remove the pan from the heat and stir with a fork. Leave to stand for 4 minutes, stir again and drain, reserving 5 tablespoons of the stock for later.

3 To serve, lift the salmon out of the steamer, remove the plastic wrap and pour all the juices into the noodles. Add the retained stock and coriander and mix well. Divide between four bowls and place a salmon fillet and some of the vegetables on top of each.

56 Poached Salmon with Asian Noodle Salad

Hot and spicy

Preparation time 20 minutes, plus marinating time

Serves 4

175 g (6 oz) rice vermicelli or Thai stir-fry rice noodles

1 teaspoon light sesame oil

1 red pepper, seeded and finely shredded

4 green onions, finely shredded

15 cm (6 inch) piece cucumber, peeled, seeded and finely sliced

450 g (1 lb) cold poached salmon (see pages 12–13)

50 g (2 oz) fresh coriander, roughly chopped

FOR THE DRESSING:

4 tablespoons Thai fish sauce (*nam pla*)

4 tablespoons fresh lime juice

1/2 teaspoon dried chili flakes

1 1/2 teaspoons sugar

1 garlic clove, finely crushed

This dish is dedicated to all those who think salads are boring. Packed full of fantastic textures and flavors, it is a true taste sensation. I like to use vermicelli noodles as they soak up the sauce. They also provide a great texture contrast to the crunch of the pepper, green onions and cucumber. This salad really does benefit from being made a couple of hours in advance to allow the flavors to develop.

1 Cook or soak the noodles according to the packet instructions. Drain well and toss with the sesame oil.

2 Mix the dressing ingredients together. Toss the red pepper, green onions and cucumber into the noodles with 6 tablespoons of the dressing.

3 Flake the salmon and fold through the noodles. Cover and leave for about 2 hours to absorb all the flavors.

4 Mix in the coriander and divide the noodles between four plates. Spoon the rest of the dressing around the edge of each plate and serve.

57 Herb Risotto with Sliced Salmon Carpaccio

Smart entertaining
Preparation time 40 minutes
Serves 6

75 ml (¹/₃ cup) olive oil

1 onion, finely chopped

450 g (1 lb) risotto rice (arborio, carnaroli, vialone or nano)

150 ml (²/₃ cup) dry white wine

about 1.5 liters (2³/₄ pints) hot vegetable or chicken stock

freshly ground sea salt and freshly ground black pepper

25 g (2 tablespoons) butter

4–6 tablespoons chopped fresh mixed herbs (parsley, basil, thyme, chervil)

85 g (³/₄ cup) Parmesan cheese, grated

350 g (12 oz) very fresh salmon fillet, cut across into thin strips

a squeeze of lemon juice

The idea for this was 'borrowed' from the menu of the magnificent San Pietro di Positano Hotel on the Amalfi coast in Italy. There they used sea bass in the dish, and I was delighted by the way the heat of the risotto had just started to cook the fish and no more. As I was eating, I had a flash of inspiration – I just knew it would work with thin slices of salmon. On my return home it was the first dish I cooked, and – wouldn't you know it? – the Scottish salmon seemed to combine with the risotto with finer results than the Italian sea bass!

1 Heat the olive oil in a large saucepan and add the onion. Cook gently for 3–5 minutes until soft. Add the rice and stir until well coated with oil. Pour in the wine and boil hard to reduce until almost disappeared.

2 Begin to add the hot stock a large ladleful at a time, stirring until each ladleful is absorbed into the rice. Continue until the rice is tender and creamy, but the grains still firm. (This should take about 30 minutes, depending on the type of rice used.)

3 Taste the risotto and season well with salt and lots of freshly ground black pepper. Beat in the butter, herbs and Parmesan. The risotto should be nice and creamy as the starch in the rice will have thickened the stock, and the butter and Parmesan will have given it a nice gloss.

4 Ladle into warmed shallow bowls, quickly lay the salmon strips over the top and squeeze over the lemon juice – carry the bowls straight to the table before the salmon cooks through!

58 Risotto of Salmon, Peas and Bacon

Informal supper
Preparation time 45 minutes
Serves 4

60 ml (4 tablespoons) olive oil

130 g (4.5 oz) pack *cubetti di pancetta*, or smoked streaky bacon, cubed

1 onion, finely chopped

1 garlic clove, finely chopped

225 g (1 3/4 cups) risotto rice, such as arborio

200 ml (3/4 cup) dry white wine

about 850 ml (1 1/2 pints) hot chicken stock

50 g (1/4 cup) butter

50 g (1/2 cup) Parmesan cheese, finely grated, plus extra to serve (optional)

225 g (8 oz) salmon fillet, cut into 1 cm (1/2 inch) cubes

175 g (1 cup) peas, fresh or frozen, thawed

2–3 tablespoons chopped fresh mint, plus extra to serve (optional)

freshly ground sea salt and freshly ground black pepper

Another risotto, but with quite a different feel to it – more robust than the preceding recipe. I've always been a fan of that great standby – frozen peas. I recommend the small and sweet Bird's Eye Petits Pois here, along with either diced streaky bacon or a packet of Italian pancetta lardons (*cubetti*) that are increasingly available in supermarkets, and Orkney salmon. Thus equipped, you will be able to prepare a risotto where the salty bacon contrasts with the sweet peas, providing as fitting an accompaniment for juicy chunks of Orkney salmon as you're likely to find.

1 Heat the olive oil in a large pan. Add the bacon, onion and garlic and stir-fry over a medium heat until the bacon has lightly browned and the onion has become translucent.

2 Add the rice and stir it around for a couple of minutes until it is well coated in the oil. Add the white wine and simmer for another 4–5 minutes, stirring, until almost all the liquid has been absorbed by the rice.

3 Begin to add the hot stock a large ladleful at a time, stirring until each ladleful is absorbed into the rice. Continue until the rice is tender and creamy, but the grains still firm. (This should take about 30 minutes, depending on the type of rice used.)

4 Beat in the butter and Parmesan with a wooden spoon until glossy, rich and creamy. Now add the salmon and peas, cook over a very low heat for another 3 minutes and then stir in the mint. The risotto should take about 40 minutes in total to cook.

5 Check the seasoning, spoon into four warmed serving bowls and sprinkle with a little more cheese and a bit more chopped mint if you wish.

NB The resulting risotto should be slightly runny and fall back to its own level in the pan. If it's too thick, just add some hot water.

59 Char-grilled Salmon with Herb Risotto Cake

Prepare in advance
Preparation time 45 minutes
Serves 4

4 tablespoons olive oil, plus extra for brushing

1 small onion, finely chopped

1 garlic clove, finely chopped

225 g (1 3/4 cups) arborio or other risotto rice

150 ml (2/3 cup) dry white wine

about 850 ml (1 1/4 pints) hot vegetable or fish stock

4 tablespoons chopped fresh mixed herbs (parsley, basil, thyme, chervil)

50 g (1/2 cup) Parmesan cheese, finely grated

freshly ground sea salt and freshly ground black pepper

1 medium egg, beaten

flour, for dusting

butter, for frying

4 × 115 g (4 oz) salmon fillets

rocket leaves, to serve

1 quantity Green Mayonnaise (see page 17)

I always seem to make far too much risotto, but this is never a cause for concern for me, as I know how easy it is to convert leftover risotto into risotto cakes. Here I've taken it one step further and split the cake in two horizontally, and sandwiched a piece of seared salmon in between with a handful of rocket.

1 Heat the olive oil in a large pan. Add the onion and garlic and stir-fry over a medium heat until the onion has become translucent. Add the rice and stir for a couple of minutes until it is well coated in the oil. Add the white wine and simmer for 4–5 minutes, stirring, until almost all the liquid has been absorbed by the rice.

2 Add half the stock and bring up to the boil, stirring all the time. Reduce the heat to a simmer and leave the risotto to cook until the stock has been absorbed. Add the rest of the stock and continue to cook, stirring occasionally, until the rice is tender – a bit softer than for a normal risotto – and the texture is thick, rich and creamy. This should take about 30 minutes in all.

3 Add the chopped herbs and Parmesan and season to taste with salt and pepper. Cook for 2 minutes. Allow to cool for a minute or two, then beat in the egg. Spread the mixture out on to a tray until cool enough to handle.

4 Divide the rice into four and roll into balls, then flatten into 'burger' shapes. Place on a baking tray and leave to firm up in the fridge for 30 minutes. When firm, dust lightly in seasoned flour. Melt a little butter in a non-stick frying pan and fry the risotto cakes for about 3 minutes on each side until golden. Keep warm in the oven while you cook the salmon.

5 Heat a ribbed grill pan until hot. Brush the salmon fillets with a little olive oil, char-grill them (see page 12) and season.

6 Carefully split the risotto cakes in two horizontally, place one half on a plate, top with some rocket leaves, then a piece of salmon, and then the remaining piece of risotto cake – there you have a sophisticated salmon burger. Serve with the Green Mayonnaise and dressed rocket leaves.

60 Hot-smoked Salmon Kedgeree

Informal supper
Preparation time 30 minutes
Serves 4

175 g (heaped 1 cup) long-grain rice

85 g ($^1/_3$ cup) butter

225 g (8 oz) large cherry tomatoes, halved

1 bunch green onions, chopped

1 tablespoon mild curry paste

350 g (12 oz) hot-smoked salmon, skinned and flaked

freshly ground sea salt and freshly ground black pepper

4 soft-boiled eggs

3 tablespoons chopped fresh parsley or coriander

1 large fresh red chili, seeded and chopped

Hot-smoked salmon could have been created for kedgeree, so well does its flavor marry with the long-grain rice, eggs and the gentle spicing of this Anglo/Indian creation. Kedgeree was traditionally eaten for breakfast, but I prefer to eat it once the sun's over the yard arm (an old nautical expression, meaning I like it for my supper).

1 Cook the rice according to the packet instructions or boil in salted water until tender. Drain well.

2 Melt the butter in a large sauté pan and add the halved tomatoes, cut-side down. Cook over a brisk heat for 2–3 minutes without moving them, then turn over, add the chopped green onions and cook for 1 minute. Stir in the curry paste to coat, followed by the rice and the salmon, cook until warmed through and season to taste. Tip on to a large warm serving dish.

3 Peel the eggs, cut into quarters and arrange over the kedgeree. Scatter with chopped parsley or coriander and chili and serve while still hot.

61 Salmon Pilaff with Saffron, Raisins and Pine Nuts

Informal supper
Preparation time 25 minutes
Serves 4

50 g (¼ cup) butter

50 g (6 tablespoons) pine nuts

1 large onion, thinly sliced

5 cm (2 inch) piece fresh ginger, peeled and chopped

225 g (1¾ cups) long-grain rice

50 g (3 tablespoons) raisins

finely grated rind of 1 orange

a good pinch of cinnamon

2 whole cloves

1 teaspoon saffron threads

freshly ground sea salt and freshly ground black pepper

700 ml–1 liter (1¼–1¾ pints) boiling fish or vegetable stock

550 g (1 lb 4 oz) salmon fillet, skinned and cut into large cubes

4 tablespoons chopped fresh mint

A pilaff is a rice dish originating from the eastern Mediterranean (Turkey to be exact), but I have encountered many variations. My rendition features raisins, pine nuts and saffron: all flavorings which combine well with salmon. For me, one of the main attractions of the pilaff is that it's a one-pot dish, which minimizes the washing up. The secret of success lies in getting the ratio of rice to stock just spot on – if in doubt, err on the dry side; you can always add a bit more liquid, but drying out a soggy pilaff is an impossible task.

1 Preheat the oven to 180°C/350°F.

2 Melt the butter in an ovenproof dish and cook the pine nuts until golden (watch out: they can burn), then lift them out with a slotted spoon. Add the onion and ginger to the pan and cook until golden and soft – about 15 minutes.

3 Add the rice to the dish and stir well to coat. Add the raisins, orange rind, cinnamon, cloves and saffron threads. Cook for a couple of minutes and season well. Level off the rice and pour over enough boiling stock to cover. Cover the pilaff with a lid or foil and bake in the oven for 15 minutes.

4 Uncover the pilaff and stir in the cubed salmon. Re-cover and return to the oven for another 5 minutes. Remove from the oven, uncover and scatter with the pine nuts and chopped mint. Serve immediately.

62 Pancetta-wrapped Salmon with Mushroom and Barley Risotto

Smart entertaining
Preparation time 30 minutes
Serves 4

4 × 115 g (4 oz) salmon fillets

freshly ground sea salt and freshly ground black pepper

8–12 slices pancetta

3 tablespoons olive oil, plus extra for drizzling

175 g (heaped 1 cup) pearl barley, washed and drained

1 small onion, finely chopped

1 garlic clove, finely chopped

425 ml (1³/₄ cups) chicken or vegetable stock or water

1 tablespoon light soy sauce

150 ml (²/₃ cup) red wine

225 g (8 oz) chanterelles (or other mushrooms, such as ceps, porcini, field mushrooms or large flat mushrooms)

50 g (¹/₄ cup) unsalted butter

1 tablespoon each chopped fresh tarragon and parsley

This dish has a strong autumnal feel to it, and features a version of risotto made using pearl barley. The correct name for this would be (I guess) 'barlotto.' To make serving this dish easier I would suggest making the 'barlotto' in advance and reheating it, something it does well as, unlike rice, barley doesn't go soggy with keeping. Try to find the really thin Italian pancetta to wrap the salmon in, or, failing that, thin streaky bacon. If you are making this in the autumn do try to find some 'real' wild mushrooms, such as ceps or chanterelles, rather than the cultivated ones, which don't have as good a flavor.

1 Preheat the oven to 220°C/425°F.

2 Season the salmon fillets with salt and pepper and then wrap each in 2–3 slices of the pancetta. Cover and set aside.

3 Heat a large frying pan until hot. Pour in the olive oil, then add the barley and stir until it starts to turn golden – about 5 minutes. Add the onion and garlic and continue frying for 5–10 minutes, until the barley starts to brown. Don't let it burn. Add the stock, soy sauce, red wine and seasoning. Bring to the boil and simmer gently until nearly all the liquid is gone – this should take at least 30 minutes.

4 Meanwhile, brush or scrape the mushrooms clean (slicing any bigger ones to size) and heat another frying pan until it's hot. Add 25 g (2 tablespoons) of the butter and the mushrooms. Stir-fry until lightly colored – about 4–5 minutes. Season with salt and pepper. Add the stir-fried mushrooms to the barley and mix together. Remove from the heat and cover with tin foil pierced with holes to allow the barley to swell and absorb all the liquid. Leave it in a warm place for 15 minutes. (At this stage, you could let the 'barlotto' cool, reheating it for serving up to 24 hours later.)

5 Whilst waiting for the 'barlotto' to rest, place the pancetta-wrapped salmon on a baking tray, drizzle with olive oil and bake for approximately 10 minutes until the pancetta is golden.

6 Pop the 'barlotto' pan back on the heat, add the tarragon and parsley, and the remaining butter. Stir well until hot, taste for seasoning and divide between four plates. Carve each fillet into three slices, place on top of the 'barlotto' and serve.

63 Char-grilled Salmon and Roast Vegetable Couscous

Smart entertaining
Preparation time 30 minutes
Serves 4

1 eggplant, sliced lengthways, salted and allowed to drain

2 medium zucchini, sliced lengthways into four

1 red pepper, halved, seeded and cut into 4 strips

3 tablespoons olive oil, plus extra for brushing

freshly ground sea salt and freshly ground black pepper

250 g (1 1/2 cups) couscous

2 tablespoons chopped fresh coriander

juice of 1 lemon

4 × 140 g (5 oz) salmon fillets

1 quantity Sauce Vierge (see page 14)

This is one of my dinner party staples, as it's a classy-looking dish that tastes great – and most of the work is done ahead of serving. Make the couscous in advance, and either reheat in the oven, or, even better, in a microwave. I like to serve it with Sauce Vierge – the base can be ready for last-minute finishing, leaving you free to concentrate on cooking the salmon. Either char-grill the fillets or, if you're looking for an easy time, bake them in the oven. If baking, I usually spoon the sauce over the salmon, as its appearance is never as good as when it's got a nice bit of color from a hot frying pan.

1 Heat a ribbed grill pan until hot. Brush all the vegetables with olive oil and add to the grill pan in batches. Char-grill for about 5 minutes on each side until each strip has grill marks on it and is nice and tender. Remove from the pan, season with salt and pepper, and set aside.

2 To make the couscous, pour 300 ml (1/2 pint) boiling water over the grains and cover with plastic wrap. After 5 minutes, remove the plastic wrap and, using a fork, fluff up the grains so that they separate. Now dice the char-grilled vegetables and stir through the couscous with the freshly chopped coriander, olive oil, lemon juice and seasoning.

3 Reheat the grill pan and brush with a little olive oil. Meanwhile, season the salmon fillets. Place the fillets on the grill and char-grill for 2–3 minutes each side. Don't be tempted to fiddle with them: you are looking to get nice dark grill lines on the fillets.

4 Divide the couscous between four serving plates and top each with a char-grilled salmon fillet. Spoon around the Sauce Vierge and serve.

64 Oatmeal-crusted Salmon with Mustard Sauce

Informal supper
Preparation time 25 minutes
Serves 4

450 g (1 lb) new potatoes

450 g (1 lb 2 oz) kale

4 × 140 g (5 oz) salmon tail fillets

freshly ground sea salt and freshly ground black pepper

2 tablespoons Dijon mustard

115 g (1 1/4 cups) pinhead oatmeal

butter or olive oil, for frying

1 quantity Mustard Sauce (see page 24), warmed through

Frying in oatmeal is a traditional Scottish technique normally associated with herring. Salmon fillets make a fine replacement, with the added advantage that you don't have to contend with the herring's fiddly bones. The idea is to get the oatmeal nice and crispy to form a crunchy crust around the soft salmon center. The mustard sauce provides the perfect counterpoint, and kale (a vastly under-rated vegetable) continues the Scottish theme.

1 Cook the potatoes in simmering, salted water, for approximately 20 minutes, until tender. Add the kale to a large pot of boiling, salted water and simmer gently for 10 minutes or until tender.

2 Meanwhile, season the salmon with salt and pepper. Rub the salmon on both sides with the mustard. Dip the fish in the oatmeal to coat both sides.

3 Melt a little butter in a non-stick frying pan and gently fry the fish, turning once until lightly browned on each side – about 7–8 minutes in all.

4 Serve straight from the pan with the boiled potatoes, cooked curly kale and Mustard Sauce.

65 Thai Green Salmon Curry

Hot and spicy
Preparation time 35 minutes
Serves 4

4 tablespoons sunflower oil

1 onion, finely chopped

1 red pepper, seeded and sliced

6 tablespoons bought Thai green curry paste, or fresh (see below)

2 × 400 ml (14 fl oz) cans coconut milk

400 ml (1²/₃ cups) vegetable stock or water

3 kaffir lime leaves

175 g (6 oz) small broccoli florets

85 g (3 oz) mange tout

2 zucchini, sliced

2 tablespoons chopped fresh basil, plus extra to garnish

2 tablespoons chopped fresh coriander

freshly ground sea salt and freshly ground black pepper

450 g (1 lb) salmon fillet, cut into medallions (see pages 10–11)

1 quantity Perfect Basmati Rice (see page 97)

This is a wonderfully aromatic curry that is a perfect accompaniment for salmon. The addition of kaffir lime leaves and loads of herbs makes it really fragrant. Serve with plenty of Perfect Basmati Rice (see page 97) to soak up the sauce.

1 Heat 3 tablespoons of the oil in a large sauté pan until smoking, then add the sliced onion and red pepper. Cook over a high heat until the onion is just beginning to catch and go brown around the edges.

2 Stir in the curry paste, cook for 1 minute, and add the coconut milk, stock and lime leaves. Bring to the boil then turn down the heat and simmer gently for 10 minutes.

3 Add the broccoli and simmer for 5 minutes, then add the mange tout and zucchini and simmer for a further 5 minutes or until the vegetables are tender and the sauce slightly thickened. Stir in the basil and coriander and season to taste.

4 Meanwhile, heat the remaining sunflower oil in a medium non-stick frying pan and add the salmon medallions. Cook for 1–2 minutes on one side only, resisting the temptation to move them around – you want a nice caramelized crust on them. Once the raw side starts to change color, remove the medallions and place on a baking tray.

5 Divide the curry among four warmed deep soup bowls, placing three or four medallions of salmon on top of each. Serve with Perfect Basmati Rice.

Thai Green Curry Paste

There's nothing quite like making your own curry paste. There may seem to be a lot of ingredients, but a food processor makes light work of them. Seed and chop 6 long green chilies. Roughly chop 2 stems of lemon grass and 50 g (2 oz) fresh coriander. Peel and chop 2.5 cm (1 inch) galangal or fresh ginger and 2 shallots. Peel 3 garlic cloves. Put all these ingredients in a food processor, along with 3 kaffir lime leaves, 1 teaspoon ground cumin, the finely grated rind and juice of a lime and 150 ml (²/₃ cup) vegetable, fish or chicken stock, and blitz until smooth. Don't worry if you make too much paste, as you can freeze it for another day.

66 Salmon Tempura with Lemon Rice and Chili Oil

Smart entertaining

Preparation time 25 minutes

Serves 4

FOR THE LEMON RICE:

225 g (1 3/4 cups) long-grain rice

85 g (3/4 cup) frozen peas, thawed

juice and finely grated rind of 1 lemon (reserve a little juice to season the salmon)

1 tablespoon finely chopped fresh chives

FOR THE SALMON:

225 g (8 oz) salmon fillet, cut into medallions (see pages 10–11)

freshly ground sea salt and freshly ground black pepper

sunflower oil, for deep-frying

a little flour, for coating

home-made Chili Oil (see page 123) or ready-made chili oil, to serve

sprigs of fresh coriander, to garnish (optional)

FOR THE TEMPURA BATTER:

50 g (6 tablespoons) all-purpose flour

50 g (6 tablespoons) cornstarch

ice-cold fizzy mineral water

Good tempura batter should be airy, light and crunchy, without any trace of oiliness. To ensure yours ends up like this, follow these guidelines. Make the tempura batter at the last moment, sifting in the flour and then mixing it in with a fork. Don't overwork it – there should still be small lumps and traces of flour, as this is what makes the batter light. Don't overcrowd the pan when frying – fry in small batches and serve as soon as possible. Finally, this is not the traditional way to serve tempura, but it is tasty, and that's what matters!

1 To make the lemon rice, wash the rice well, drain and put into a huge pan of fast-boiling salted water. Stir the rice and boil fast for 15 minutes, until just tender, then drain well through a colander or sieve. Return to the hot pan, add the peas and mix in the lemon juice and rind and the chives. Keep warm. If you are preparing the rice in advance, leave out the chives until the last minute and reheat the rice in the microwave or oven.

2 Season the salmon with salt and pepper and a little lemon juice.

3 Put the tempura ingredients into a bowl, adding just enough mineral water to form a batter with the consistency of light cream, and give them a quick mix. There's no need to work the mixture – a quick swish with chopsticks is the traditional method, so that there is still the odd lump or two.

4 Pour the oil for deep-frying into a pan or electric deep-fat fryer until it is one-third full and heat it to 190°C/375°F (use a cooking thermometer if necessary). Dip the pieces of salmon in flour, then in the batter, and fry a few at a time for about 2 minutes until crisp and golden. You may need to turn the pieces halfway through cooking, so don't overcrowd the pan. Drain the salmon on paper towel and keep warm while you cook the rest.

5 To serve, divide the rice between four warmed serving plates. Place the salmon tempura on top and drizzle a little chili oil round the outside. A sprig of coriander works well as a garnish.

67 Hot-and-sour Salmon

Hot and spicy

Preparation time 20 minutes

Serves 4

3 tablespoons white wine vinegar

2 tablespoons light soy sauce

4 tablespoons fish or vegetable stock

2 tablespoons fresh orange juice

juice of 1 lime

2 tablespoons dry sherry

1 teaspoon cornstarch

2 tablespoons tomato paste

2 tablespoons soft brown sugar

1 tablespoon vegetable oil

2 garlic cloves, finely chopped

1 cm (1/2 inch) piece fresh ginger, peeled and chopped

2 fresh red chilies, seeded and chopped

1 medium carrot, very finely sliced

450 g (1 lb) salmon fillet, cubed

4 green onions, shredded

egg noodles and stir-fried sugar snap peas, to serve (optional)

FOR THE BASMATI RICE (OPTIONAL):

280 g (heaped 1 3/4 cups) basmati rice

1/2 teaspoon freshly ground sea salt and freshly ground black pepper

As with many dishes of Asian origin, the success of this recipe relies on getting the balance of the hot, sour, sweet and salty flavors just right. The concept is similar to sweet and sour, but with a bit more emphasis on chili heat. If you don't have time to prepare the sauce, Baxter's do a great ready-made alternative, which is available in most supermarkets.

1 To make the sauce, whisk the first six ingredients with the cornstarch, tomato paste and sugar.

2 Heat the oil in a medium pan and add the garlic, ginger and chilies. Cook for 1 minute until golden, then whisk the sauce again and pour into the pan. Bring to the boil, stirring occasionally and simmer for 2 minutes.

3 Add the carrot, salmon chunks and green onions. Simmer very gently for 2 minutes or until the salmon is cooked through. Ladle into bowls of Perfect Basmati Rice (see below) or egg noodles, and some stir-fried sugar snap peas.

Perfect Basmati Rice

To achieve consistently light, fluffy basmati rice, always wash the rice first under cold water until the water runs clear, indicating that you've got rid of most of the loose starch clinging to the rice grains. Then bring a huge pan of cold salted water (about 10 times the volume of rice) to the boil and add the rice. Bring back to a rolling boil and stir once. Boil for exactly 8 minutes. Check the rice – it should still have a slight crunch – then drain well, return to the pan and cover with a tight-fitting lid. Leave to steam in its own heat undisturbed for another 10 minutes. Don't be tempted to peek at the rice before it's ready – lifting the lid allows all the heat to escape. Use a fork to fluff up the grains and serve. Perfect rice!

68 Seared Salmon with Chili and Parmesan Polenta

Quick and easy
Preparation time 15 minutes
Serves 4

4 × 175 g (6 oz) salmon fillets, skinned

2 fresh red chilies, thinly sliced (seeds and all if you like it very hot)

85 g (¹/₂ cup) quick-cook polenta

50 g (¹/₄ cup) butter

50 g (¹/₂ cup) Parmesan cheese, grated

3 tablespoons chopped parsley

freshly ground sea salt and freshly ground black pepper

extra grated Parmesan and extra virgin olive oil, to serve

Polenta is made from dried and ground corn and is usually served in one of two ways – either it's served 'wet,' a bit like porridge, or it's allowed to set and then cut into shapes and fried. Personally I think that a dollop of soft, creamy polenta flavored with butter and Parmesan is the best partner to a nice piece of seared salmon. The addition of chili is a personal favorite but could easily be omitted.

1 Heat a non-stick frying pan until searing hot and add the salmon fillets, skinned-side down first. Cook without moving for 2–3 minutes, then flip over, turn down the heat and cook for a further 2–3 minutes until cooked through but still moist. Lift out of the pan and on to a plate to keep warm while you make the polenta.

2 Put the chilies into 450 ml (1 ³/₄ cups) water and bring to the boil, then shower in the polenta, stirring all the time. Cook for 4 minutes, then beat in the butter, Parmesan, parsley and plenty of seasoning. Quickly spoon on to four warmed plates and top each with a salmon fillet. Serve with extra grated Parmesan and olive oil for drizzling.

NB If you let the polenta stand for too long it will thicken up – just beat in a little more hot water to loosen it.

69 Baked Salmon with Shrimp and Ginger Cream

Quick and easy

Preparation time 15 minutes

Serves 4

4 × 175 g (6 oz) salmon fillets or salmon darnes (see pages 10–11)

40 g (3 tablespoons) butter

juice of 1 lemon

freshly ground sea salt and freshly ground black pepper

3 cm (1 1/4 inch) piece fresh ginger, peeled and cut into fine julienne (matchsticks)

300 ml (1 1/4 cups) 35% cream

225 g (8 oz) fresh cooked peeled shrimp

3 tablespoons chopped fresh coriander and chives

1 quantity Perfect Basmati Rice (see page 97)

1 quantity Wilted Greens (see page 123)

This dish gives loads of flavor for minimum effort. The fresh zingy flavor of ginger prevents what is quite a rich dish from becoming cloying and heavy. Be careful not to overcook the shrimp: they just need to be warmed through in the ginger cream, which can be prepared ahead if you want to save time.

1 Preheat the oven to 190°C/375°F. Lay the salmon in a baking tray. Dot with 25 g (2 tablespoons) of the butter, squeeze over some lemon juice and season well. Bake for 7–8 minutes, depending on the thickness.

2 While the salmon is baking, sweat the ginger in the remaining butter for 5 minutes to soften. Pour the cream over the ginger and season well. Bring the cream to the boil and simmer for 2 minutes until slightly thickened. Stir in the shrimp, a good squeeze of lemon juice and the chopped herbs.

3 Lift the salmon off the baking tray onto four warmed plates. Pour the juices into the cream sauce and mix well. Check the seasoning, then pour over the salmon, ensuring you divide the shrimp equally. Serve with Perfect Basmati Rice and some Wilted Greens.

70 Seared Salmon with Curried Lentils

Smart entertaining
Preparation time 25 minutes
Serves 4

225 g (8 oz) Puy or continental lentils

2 tablespoons sunflower oil, plus extra for frying

1 small carrot, very finely diced

1 celery stick, finely diced

1 small leek, finely diced

1 garlic clove, finely chopped

2 cm (³/4 inch) piece fresh ginger, peeled and finely diced

1 teaspoon mild curry paste

freshly ground sea salt and freshly ground black pepper

300 ml (1¹/4 cups) chicken stock

3 tomatoes, diced

3 tablespoons chopped fresh coriander

4 × 140 g (5 oz) salmon fillets

a squeeze of lemon juice

4 tablespoons crème fraîche

I've always loved the combination of earthy lentils and the spicy aromatic flavors of curry spicing. Add a piece of seared salmon and you've got a superb dinner party dish that's tasty, nutritious and can be prepared in advance. I prefer the flavor of the small, dark, slaty-green Puy lentils, but recently I've found variable quality. In their place I've been using green or brown 'continental' lentils with much success. Avoid the orange type for this dish, as they are really suitable only for cooking to a purée or making soup.

1 Cook the lentils in plenty of boiling water for 15–20 minutes or until tender. Drain in a sieve and spread on a tray to dry.

2 Warm the sunflower oil in a saucepan and sweat the carrot, celery, leek, garlic and ginger for approximately 10 minutes, until soft. Add the curry paste and some seasoning and cook for 2–3 minutes. Stir in the lentils, then add the stock and bring to the boil. Add the tomatoes and 2 tablespoons of the chopped coriander. Check the seasoning. Simmer for 30 seconds, or until you have a loose sauce. Remove from the heat and keep warm.

3 Put a small drop of sunflower oil in a hot frying pan, add the salmon fillets and fry for 2–3 minutes on each side. Season with salt, pepper and lemon juice.

4 Stir the crème fraîche into the lentils, and ladle into four warmed serving bowls. Top with the seared salmon and garnish with the remaining coriander.

71 Salmon Fishcakes with Lemon Butter Sauce

Prepare in advance

Preparation time 30 minutes, plus freezing time

Serves 6

50 g (¼ cup) unsalted butter

450 g (1 lb) salmon fillet, skinned

juice of 1 lemon

freshly ground sea salt and freshly ground black pepper

1 teaspoon home-made Chili Oil (see page 123) or ready-made chili oil

225 g (1 cup) cooked mashed potatoes

3 green onions, finely chopped

3 tablespoon chopped fresh herbs (parsley and coriander for preference)

Thai fish sauce (*nam pla*)

115 g (¾ cup) all-purpose flour

4 eggs

115 g (1 cup) fresh breadcrumbs

sunflower oil, for frying

1 quantity Lemon Butter Sauce (see page 20)

Everybody should be able to make a good fishcake – mastering this sublime combination of fish and mash arms you with one of the most versatile dishes around. It can star as a dinner party starter, provide the perfect lunch or nourish your soul as a comfort food. To my mind, salmon makes the best fishcake of all, and the best accompaniment to a salmon fishcake is a sharp, silky lemon butter sauce.

1 Preheat the oven to 230°C/450°F.

2 Use half the butter to grease a roasting pan big enough to hold the salmon fillets comfortably. Dot the remaining butter over the fish in small lumps. Pour the lemon juice over and add salt, pepper and the chili oil.

3 Bake the fish for approximately 5 minutes until just cooked; it should be slightly undercooked in the center. Once out of the oven, let the fish stand for 5 minutes, then flake into bite-sized pieces.

4 Put the mashed potatoes (these can be hot or cold) into a large mixing bowl and add the salmon, green onions and herbs. Fold together with a wooden spoon until the fish is well mixed through. Taste and season with a splash of Thai fish sauce, salt and pepper.

5 Cover a household tray (either tin or plastic) with greaseproof paper, then, using your hands, shape the mix into 6 fishcakes of about 115 g (4 oz) each. Place the fishcakes on the tray, cover with another sheet of greaseproof paper, then lightly cover in plastic wrap. Put them in the freezer overnight and allow them to freeze hard.

5 Prepare three shallow trays thus: sift the flour into the first tray; beat the eggs with a pinch of salt into the second tray; half fill the third tray with breadcrumbs. Remove the frozen fishcakes from the freezer. Add 2 or 3 fishcakes to the first tray and coat them with flour, shaking off any excess. Transfer them to the second tray and coat well in the egg. Finally, place them into the breadcrumbs, covering them thoroughly. Repeat the process with the other cakes. Refreeze them if not serving immediately.

6 To serve, preheat the oven to 120°C/250°F. Heat a small frying pan until hot, then fill it one-third full with oil and allow it to heat for 1–2 minutes.

Place the fishcakes in the pan and shallow-fry them for 3–4 minutes or until nicely golden in color. Turn over and repeat on the other side, then, using tongs or a spatula, place the fishcakes on to a baking sheet covered with a double layer of paper towel. Place the tray into the oven for 45 minutes. This will complete the defrosting process. They will keep warm, in a low oven, for up to an hour without spoiling. Serve with the Lemon Butter Sauce.

72 Salmon and Potato Bridies

Informal supper
Preparation time 45 minutes
Serves 4

225 g (8 oz) new potatoes, scrubbed

25 g (2 tablespoons) butter

5 tablespoons olive oil

1 medium leek, trimmed and thinly sliced

freshly ground sea salt and freshly ground black pepper

225 g (8 oz) cooked salmon (see pages 12–13)

3 tablespoons chopped fresh parsley

a squeeze of lemon juice

450 g (1 lb) fresh or frozen puff pastry, thawed

1 egg, beaten with a pinch of salt, to glaze

salad leaves, to serve

These are what I call posh Scottish pies! They're a good way to use up leftover salmon, transforming it into a tasty treat. They're delicious cold, so I find them perfect for picnics.

1 Preheat the oven to 200°C/400°F.

2 Cook the potatoes in simmering salted water for about 20 minutes until tender.

3 Meanwhile, heat the butter with 1 tablespoon of the oil in a frying pan, add the leek, toss to coat and sweat for about 7 minutes until it starts to collapse. Season with salt and pepper. Flake the salmon.

4 Drain the potatoes and place in a large mixing bowl. Add the remaining oil and gently crush each potato with the back of a fork until they just split. This is a kind of textured mash, so don't be tempted to make it too smooth. Mix carefully until all the oil has been absorbed.

5 Stir in the leek, salmon and chopped parsley. Taste and season with salt, pepper and a squeeze of lemon juice.

6 Cut the pastry in two, then roll each half out to 5 mm (1/4 inch) thick and cut out two 20 cm (8 inch) circles from each half – use a round plate as a template. Place a quarter of the filling in the middle of each circle of pastry. Brush the edges with water and pull up to enclose the filling. Pinch together and crimp the central edge with your fingers. Brush with beaten egg and make a couple of holes in the top.

7 Place on a baking sheet and bake for 20 minutes until puffed and golden brown. Serve hot or cold with a green salad.

73 Hot-smoked Salmon Hash with Spicy Sausage and Poached Egg

Informal supper
Preparation time 30 minutes
Serves 4

600 g (1 lb 5 oz) floury potatoes

freshly ground sea salt and freshly ground black pepper

4 tablespoons olive oil

25 g (2 tablespoons) butter

1 medium onion, chopped

175 g (6 oz) chorizo, diced

225 g (8 oz) hot-smoked salmon, flaked

1 bunch watercress, roughly chopped

3 tablespoons grated Parmesan

4 poached eggs (see page 50)

I use my dad's home-grown Red Duke of York potatoes for this brunch recipe (you could use some other floury variety like King Edward). This type of potato breaks up into floury chunks and really crisps up in the bottom of the pan. I've added Spanish chorizo sausage for a bit of spice and color – it goes so well with hot-smoked salmon.

1 Boil the potatoes whole and in their skins in plenty of salted water until just tender. This can take 20–30 minutes depending on the size – don't worry if they begin to break up. Drain and allow to steam in the sieve or colander.

2 Meanwhile, heat a large frying pan or sauté pan and swirl in the oil, then add the butter. Add the onion and cook over a medium heat for about 5 minutes until golden, then add the chorizo and cook for 2–3 minutes until the fat begins to run.

3 Now add the potatoes and crush into the pan with a fork, mixing with the onion and chorizo. Cook over a brisk heat, stirring from time to time, so that the potato begins to brown on the bottom of the pan.

4 Once the potato is golden and crisp in parts, give it a gentle stir, adding the salmon and watercress and seasoning and pressing lightly into the pan to form a 'cake.' After about 5 minutes, the hash is cooked, as the hot-smoked salmon just needs to be heated through. Serve either cut into wedges or spooned out of the pan, sprinkled with loads of Parmesan, and with a perfectly poached egg on top.

74 Hot-smoked Salmon, Potato Pancakes and Crème Fraîche

Informal supper
Preparation time 30 minutes
Serves 4

225 g (8 oz) hot-smoked salmon

115 g (4 oz) watercress

FOR THE PANCAKES:

350 g (12 oz) floury potatoes

2 tablespoons all-purpose flour

3 tablespoons milk

2 tablespoons 35% cream

2 medium eggs

2 tablespoons sunflower oil

FOR THE CRÈME FRAÎCHE:

4 green onions, finely chopped

115 g (1/2 cup) crème fraîche

1 teaspoon lemon juice

a few drops of Tabasco sauce

freshly ground sea salt and freshly ground black pepper

Smoked salmon with potato pancakes has become something of a modern restaurant classic, due to the great combination of flavors, texture and temperature. It also makes a very useful dinner party starter, as most of the preparation can be done in advance. In the restaurant, I cook the pancakes in blini pans that give them a uniform size. The easiest way to cook them at home, however, is to pour tablespoons of the mix into a large frying pan and cook them in small batches, like drop scones – don't worry if the pancakes aren't perfectly round; I think this gives them a nice home-made feel – or as one large pancake, which can be divided into four once cooked.

1 Preheat the oven to 200°C/400°F.

2 First make the pancakes. Peel the potatoes and cook them in boiling salted water until tender, then drain well and mash. Beat in the flour with a wooden spoon, add the milk and cream and mix well. Beat in the eggs, season and work it all through a sieve to remove any lumps.

3 Heat the sunflower oil in a 20 cm (8 inch) ovenproof frying pan until hot, then pour in the pancake mixture. It should be about 1 cm (1/2 inch) thick. As soon as it starts to bubble and brown around the edges, put the frying pan into the top of the hot oven and leave for 10 minutes or until cooked through. Alternatively, make 4 smaller pancakes one after the other and grill them to finish.

4 Make the green onion crème fraîche by mixing together the green onions, crème fraîche, lemon juice, Tabasco and seasoning.

5 Remove the large pancake or the four smaller ones from the oven using a thick pair of oven gloves. Each pancake should be well risen and lightly browned on top, and will keep in a warm place for 20–30 minutes.

6 To serve, quarter the pancake, if necessary, and place on four warmed plates. Put a pile of hot-smoked salmon on each pancake, followed by a good spoonful of the crème fraîche, and top with the watercress.

Potato Rösti with Poached Salmon and Green Mayonnaise

Smart entertaining
Preparation time 25 minutes
Serves 4

450 g (1 lb) potatoes (such as Golden Wonder or Kerr's Pink)

freshly ground sea salt and freshly ground black pepper

3 tablespoons olive oil, plus extra if required

4 × 175 g (6 oz) salmon fillets, skinned

1 quantity Green Mayonnaise (see page 17)

chopped fresh herbs, to serve

A rösti is a sort of pancake made from grated potato; it should be crisp and golden on the outside and soft and moist within. The easiest way to make rösti at home is to produce one large one, covering the base of a frying pan, and then cut it into wedges. Selecting the correct potato variety is the key to success – look for a floury type with a low water content, ideally Golden Wonder or Kerr's Pink, but good King Edward or Maris Piper potatoes can also give excellent results. It is important to wring as much water as possible from the grated potato prior to eating, to prevent the rösti from becoming soggy. And be careful not to get the frying pan too hot, as this can produce a rösti which is burnt on the outside yet still raw within – not recommended.

1 First make the rösti. Peel the potatoes and coarsely grate on to a clean tea towel. Roll the tea towel into a sausage shape and twist the ends to squeeze out all the moisture. Do this in batches. Put the potato into a bowl as you go and season with a teaspoon of salt and some pepper.

2 Heat the oil in a 25 cm (10 inch) frying pan. Add the potato mix and press it down evenly with the back of a spatula. If the potato absorbs all the oil, you may need to add some more. Fry over a low to medium heat for about 10–15 minutes until you can see traces of color at the edges. Using a spatula, flip it over and cook for another 10–15 minutes until golden. Now you can either keep the rösti warm, or leave to cool and reheat later in the oven at 180°C/350°F for 5 minutes.

3 Fill a wide shallow pan with cold water and add a pinch or two of salt. Slip in the salmon fillets and gradually bring the water to just below boiling point, then turn off the heat and leave the salmon for 10–15 minutes, by which time the fillets will be cooked (depending on their thickness).

4 Lift the salmon fillets out of the poaching liquid and drain on paper towel. Serve a wedge of rösti with a salmon fillet placed on top, a tablespoon of Green Mayonnaise and a dusting of chopped herbs.

Hot-smoked Salmon Fishcakes with Tomato Salsa

| Prepare in advance |
| Preparation time 20 minutes |
| Serves 8 as a starter, or 4 as a main course |

300 g (1 1/4 cups) mashed potatoes (made with King Edward or Maris Piper)

600 g (1 lb 5 oz) hot-smoked or kiln-roasted salmon, flaked

2 green onions, chopped or sliced

juice of 1 lemon

freshly ground sea salt and freshly ground black pepper

seasoned flour, for coating

butter, for frying

extra olive oil, for drizzling

FOR THE TOMATO SALSA:

6 ripe plum tomatoes, cut into eighths

1/2 red onion, finely chopped

1 garlic clove, finely chopped

2 fresh red chilies, finely sliced (seeds and all)

4 tablespoons olive oil

juice of 1 lime

4 tablespoons roughly chopped fresh coriander

This recipe varies from the classic salmon fishcake recipe on page 102, not only in that it uses hot-smoked salmon in place of poached salmon, but also because the fishcakes aren't coated in breadcrumbs and shallow-fried. In this recipe they are simply tossed in seasoned flour and fried in a little butter. This produces a thicker, darker crust, and requires a slightly dryer fish and potato mix. As the finished fishcakes are slightly drier in texture, I like to serve them with a juicy tomato salsa made from ripe plum tomatoes.

1 To make the salsa, mix all the ingredients together, cover and set aside while you make the fishcakes.

2 Put the mashed potatoes (hot or cold) into a large mixing bowl, then add the flaked salmon and green onions. Squeeze the lemon juice into the mix. Fold together with a wooden spoon until the fish is well mixed through. Taste and adjust the seasoning if necessary.

3 Shape the mixture into eight fishcakes. Dip each one in seasoned flour.

4 Melt the butter in a frying pan and when it's hot add the fishcakes and fry for 3–4 minutes until nicely golden in color. Turn over and repeat on the other side. Keep warm.

5 To serve, place a dollop of salsa in the center of each plate, place a fishcake on top and drizzle round a little olive oil.

Pan-fried Salmon with Braised Chicory and Olive Oil Mash

Smart entertaining
Preparation time 45 minutes
Serves 4

2 fat heads of chicory

50 g (1/4 cup) butter

1/2 teaspoon superfine granulated sugar

150 ml (2/3 cup) vegetable stock

450 g (1 lb) floury potatoes (such as King Edward), peeled and chopped

3 tablespoons milk

100 ml (6 tablespoons) olive oil, plus extra to serve

freshly ground sea salt and freshly ground black pepper

4 × 150 g (5 oz) salmon fillets

a squeeze of lemon juice

There seem to be several types of bitter lettuce going by the name 'chicory.' To avoid confusion, what I'm referring to here is the bundle of white and yellow elongated leaves in the shape of a fat crayon (about 10–15 cm/4–6 inches long). Eaten raw, chicory has a strong, bitter flavor, but when it's braised, the flavor mellows and the texture softens and it is delicious with salmon.

1 Preheat the oven to 190°C/375°F.

2 Halve the chicory lengthways. Melt the butter and sugar in a heavy ovenproof pan and add the chicory cut-side down. Cook over a medium heat for at least 15 minutes until golden brown and caramelized. Pour in the stock, bring to the boil and carefully place in the oven for 20–30 minutes until meltingly tender. Keep warm.

3 Meanwhile, cook the potatoes in simmering salted water until tender, then drain and mash well. Add the milk and beat in 85 ml (1/3 cup) olive oil, taste and season. Cover the mash with a butter wrapper to stop it drying out.

4 Heat a frying pan until very hot and add the remaining oil. Cook the salmon for 2–3 minutes, then turn over and repeat. The salmon should be slightly pink, and tender inside. Season with salt and pepper and a squeeze of lemon juice.

5 Place a mound of mash on each warmed plate and top with a piece of chicory, followed by the salmon and a drizzle of olive oil around the plate to finish.

Seared Salmon, Crushed Potatoes and Caviar Butter Sauce

Smart entertaining
Preparation time 35 minutes
Serves 4

450 g (1 lb) new potatoes, scrubbed

85 ml (¹/₃ cup) olive oil

freshly ground sea salt and freshly ground black pepper

3 tablespoons chopped fresh basil

1 tablespoon sunflower oil

4 × 115 g (4 oz) salmon fillets

200 ml (³/4 cup) Butter Sauce (see page 20)

1 tablespoon Avruga caviar

This dish can often be found on my restaurant menu. Use best-quality new potatoes and crush them with the back of a fork, pushing just until the potato bursts – you want to keep plenty of texture while allowing the potatoes to absorb the olive oil and seasoning. I often use Avruga instead of caviar, which is herring roe and much cheaper than the real thing. Be careful not to overheat the sauce or you'll 'cook' the Avruga, and it'll lose its lovely yielding texture.

1 Cook the potatoes in simmering salted water until tender, then drain and place in a large mixing bowl. Add the olive oil and, using the back of a fork, gently crush each potato until it just splits. This is a kind of textured mash, so don't be tempted to make it too smooth. Season, then mix carefully until all the oil has been absorbed. I cover my mash with a butter wrapper to stop it drying out. Potatoes will keep warm in a very cool oven for up to 1 hour this way. When ready to serve the potatoes, stir through the chopped basil and check the seasoning.

2 Heat a large frying pan until very hot. Add the sunflower oil and fry the salmon for 2–3 minutes on each side, until a caramelized crust forms on the outside. Season on the cooked side only.

3 Have ready the Butter Sauce, and add the Avruga, gently mixing through. Make sure you don't skimp and use dyed roe here as the color will run into the sauce and the result will be a murky gray pool!

4 Place a dollop of the crushed potatoes into the center of four warmed serving plates, place a seared salmon fillet on top and pour over the caviar butter sauce.

79 Salmon in Beer Batter with Chips and Green Mayonnaise

Informal supper

Preparation time 25 minutes

Serves 4

oil, for deep-frying

900 g (2 lb) potatoes (such as Golden Wonder), peeled

4 × 175 g (6 oz) tail-end salmon fillets, skinned

freshly ground sea salt and freshly ground black pepper

225 g (1 1/2 cups) self-raising flour, plus extra for coating

300 ml (1 1/4 cups) beer

1 quantity Green Mayonnaise (see page 17)

Salmon is excellent for fish and chips, especially with crispy beer or lager batter. I use Tenant's lager in the mix, not because it makes a better batter (any old beer or lager will do), but because I enjoy drinking the left-overs! Quite often it's possible to buy salmon tails at reduced price, and this is the perfect use for them. Split a 350 g (12 oz) tail in half lengthways and you will have 2 perfect portions of salmon for deep-frying. To make up for the amount of calories in fish and chips, I always eat it with a big salad of mixed leaves.

1 Heat the oil to 180°C/350°F in an electric deep-fat fryer or large pan (use a cooking thermometer if necessary) and preheat the oven to its lowest setting.

2 While the oil is heating, cut the potatoes. I find it best to cut a slice 1 cm (1/2 inch) thick off the potato lengthways, then, using the flat side as a base, cut the potato into 1 cm (1/2 inch) slices. Then cut each slice into 1 cm (1/2 inch) slices, resulting in 1 cm (1/2 inch) square chips. Place them in a bowl of cold water until ready to cook.

3 Drain the chips and pat dry with a clean tea towel. Depending on the size of your fryer, you may have to fry them in two batches. Carefully add the chips to the hot oil and deep-fry them for 12–15 minutes until they are a lovely golden color. Lift the basket clear of the oil and shake off any excess. Tip the chips into a bowl lined with several sheets of kitchen paper and dab them dry. Put into the oven to keep warm while you prepare the salmon and batter, but don't close the oven door or the chips will go soggy. Stick a wooden spoon in the door to keep it open!

4 Season the salmon with salt and pepper and dip in the flour to coat each piece, shaking off the excess. Gradually whisk the remaining flour into the beer with a good pinch of salt until you have a thick batter – don't worry, it will puff up in the fryer.

5 Line a roasting pan with crumpled paper towel. Dip the salmon in the batter and fry in the deep-fat fryer or pan for about 5 minutes until golden brown, then lift onto the paper towel to absorb any excess oil. You may have to do this in two batches.

6 Take the chips out of the oven as soon as the fish is cooked, sprinkle with salt and serve with the crispy battered salmon and some Green Mayonnaise.

80 Baked Salmon with Champ

Informal supper
Preparation time 30 minutes
Serves 4

140 g (²/₃ cup) butter

4 × 140 g (5 oz) salmon fillets

juice of 1 lemon

freshly ground sea salt and freshly ground black pepper

450 g (1 lb) Maris Piper potatoes, peeled and quartered

75 ml (¹/₃ cup) 35% cream

8 green onions, shredded

1 quantity Chive (or Herb) Butter Sauce (see page 20), optional

This is a simple yet satisfying dish. Champ is a traditional Irish combo of mash and green onions. Normally, the green onions are shredded and added raw to the mash – I like to shred them and then soften them in a generous amount of heavy cream before adding them. This mellows the harsh, oniony flavor and gives a rich, soft mash.

1 Preheat the oven to 200°C/400°F.

2 Heavily grease a shallow baking dish with 25 g (2 tablespoons) of the butter and place the salmon fillets into it. Squeeze over the lemon juice, dot generously with 50 g (¹/₄ cup) butter and season with salt and pepper. Set aside.

3 Place the potatoes in a pan of salted cold water and bring to the boil. As soon as the water comes to the boil, reduce to a simmer and cook for about 20 minutes. While the potatoes are cooking, bake the salmon for 7 minutes.

4 Drain the potatoes in a colander and then mash really well, so that you have a smooth but airy mixture.

5 In a small pan, bring the cream and green onions to the boil, then pour onto the mash. Beat in the remaining butter, taste and season.

6 To serve, place a generous dollop of champ on each serving plate and top with the baked salmon. This would be great served with Chive (or Herb) Butter Sauce or with just a bit of butter sitting on top of the salmon to melt down on to the champ.

81 Smoked Salmon Baked Potato with Avruga and Crème Fraîche

Quick and easy
Preparation time 1 hour
Serves 4

4 medium baking potatoes

freshly ground sea salt and freshly ground black pepper

200 ml (7 fl oz) tub crème fraîche

300 g (10 oz) sliced smoked salmon

juice of 1 lemon

4 teaspoons Avruga caviar

chopped fresh chives, to garnish

This is about as posh as the humble baked potato can get – smoked salmon, sour cream and caviar is a dish for when you're feeling flush! My favorite variety of baking potato is Golden Wonder; however, it's difficult to get large Golden Wonders, and they do have a very thick, crispy skin, so I'd advise using normal bakers here. Bake them on a baking sheet and turn after 30 minutes to get a crisp, even skin. Instead of real caviar, try Avruga, a caviar substitute made from herring roe, which has an excellent flavor and texture for a fifth of the price of the real thing.

1 Preheat the oven to 200°C/400°F.

2 Wash the potatoes and prick with a fork. Place on a baking sheet on the center shelf of the oven for approximately 1 hour, until cooked.

3 Remove the potatoes from the oven and cut in half lengthways. Scoop out the fluffy potato from each half, place in a large bowl and season. Fold in the crème fraîche, taking care as the steam from the potato is hot. Spoon the filling back into the potato skins.

4 Arrange the smoked salmon slices on top, squeeze over some lemon juice and top with a teaspoon of the Avruga. Garnish with the chopped chives and serve immediately.

82 Seared Salmon with Hot Potato and Tomato Salad

Quick and easy
Preparation time 25 minutes
Serves 4

400 g (14 oz) salad potatoes (such as Anya or Charlotte)

1 garlic clove, crushed

4 tablespoons extra virgin olive oil

1 tablespoon balsamic vinegar

freshly ground sea salt and freshly ground black pepper

350 g (12 oz) cherry tomatoes, halved

25 g (1 oz) fresh basil leaves, roughly chopped

1 tablespoon sunflower oil

4 × 115 g (4 oz) salmon escalopes (see page 10)

juice of 1/2 lemon

25g (1/4 cup) Parmesan cheese shavings

I discovered how good this combination is quite accidentally when making supper at home one evening. The potatoes absorb the juices from the tomatoes, olive oil and balsamic vinegar, and provide the perfect background to a nice slice of seared salmon. I'm convinced many of the best ideas and combinations in cooking come about by accident rather than design.

1 Cook the potatoes in a pan of salted boiling water for about 20 minutes until just tender.

2 Meanwhile, mix the garlic, olive oil, balsamic vinegar and seasoning together in a mixing bowl. Add the tomatoes and basil and mix well.

3 When the potatoes are cooked, drain and cut in half and add to the tomato mix, tossing well to coat.

4 Heat the sunflower oil in a hot frying pan, add the salmon escalopes and fry for 2 minutes on one side only. Turn on to a plate, fried-side up, and season with salt, pepper and the lemon juice.

5 Add the Parmesan to the potato and tomato salad mix and divide between four serving bowls. Place a salmon escalope on top of the salad and serve.

83 Salmon and Shrimp Pie with Cheddar and Mustard Mash

Prepare in advance
Preparation time 45 minutes
Serves 6

700 ml (1 1/4 pints) milk

1 medium onion, chopped

1 bay leaf

a few whole black peppercorns

900 g (2 lb) salmon fillet, skin on

350 g (12 oz) cooked tiger shrimp tails, peeled

85 g (1/3 cup) butter

85 g (1/2 cup) flour

freshly ground sea salt and freshly ground black pepper

4 tablespoons chopped fresh parsley

FOR THE CHEDDAR AND MUSTARD MASH:

1.3 kg (3 lb) floury potatoes, peeled

85 g (1/3 cup) butter

250 ml (1 cup) milk

3 tablespoons wholegrain mustard

115 g (1 cup) mature Cheddar cheese, grated

You can't beat a good fish pie, especially one made with lightly cooked salmon and sweet shrimp, and topped with cheesy mash, which should be cooked just long enough to develop a nice crust. If your lottery numbers come up, you could replace the shrimp with langoustines or even diced lobster. Serve with a generous amount of wilted spinach – allow at least 225 g (8 oz) of leaves per person. If you've got any left-over pie, either reheat in the microwave or use it to make fishcakes.

1 Put the milk, onion, bay leaf and a couple of peppercorns into a saucepan. Bring to the boil, then simmer for 10 minutes. Turn off the heat and set aside.

2 Lay the salmon skin-side up in a roasting pan or very large frying pan. Strain the reserved milk, pour over the salmon and simmer for 5–7 minutes until just opaque. Lift the fish out of the milk and on to a plate. When it is cool enough to handle, pull off the skin and flake the salmon into large pieces, removing any bones as you go. Transfer to a large bowl and add the shrimp.

3 Melt the butter in a small pan. Stir in the flour and gradually add the flavored milk from the roasting pan. Whisk well and simmer gently for 15 minutes until thick and a little reduced. Taste and season with salt and pepper. Stir in the parsley and pour the sauce over the salmon and shrimp. Carefully mix everything together, transfer the mixture to a 1.5 liter (2 3/4 pint) pie dish and leave to cool.

4 Pre-heat the oven to 350°F/180°C.

5 Boil the potatoes in salted water until tender, drain well and mash. Beat in the butter, milk, mustard and grated Cheddar. When the fish mixture is set, spoon over the mash, piling it high on top. Bake in the oven for 30–40 minutes or until the potato is golden brown and crispy. Serve immediately.

84 Smoked Salmon and Creamy Cabbage on a Potato Scone

Informal supper
Preparation time 20 minutes
Serves 4

225 g (8 oz) smoked salmon, cut into strips

chopped fresh parsley, to serve

FOR THE POTATO SCONES:

225 g (8 oz) floury potatoes

50 g (1/4 cup) butter, plus extra for greasing and spreading

freshly ground sea salt and freshly ground black pepper

50 g (6 tablespoons) all-purpose flour

FOR THE CABBAGE:

1/2 green cabbage, very finely shredded

50 g (1/4 cup) butter

1 garlic clove, crushed

150 ml (2/3 cup) 35% cream

The mixture of cabbage and smoked salmon was 'borrowed' from Gary Rhodes after I'd watched him demonstrating it at the BBC Good Food Show at the NEC in Birmingham. I was backstage, and had a nibble at Gary's dish when it was cleared and was impressed at how well the smoked salmon partnered the cabbage. The addition of the potato scone came a couple of years later while I was experimenting with new dishes for the lunch menu at my Glasgow restaurant: another example of how some dishes evolve rather than being dreamed up out of thin air.

1 To make the scones, peel the potatoes and boil in salted water for 20 minutes or until very tender. Drain well, return to the pan and toss them around over the heat to dry them out a bit more. Mash or sieve into a bowl.

2 Beat in the butter, salt and pepper and work in the flour to make a soft dough. Turn out on to a floured board, divide in two and lightly knead each half into a smooth ball. Roll each ball out into a circle about 5 mm (1/4 inch) thick and cut each circle into four. Prick well with a fork.

3 Heat a heavy frying pan or grill, wipe with butter and cook four of the scones on each side for 3 minutes until golden brown and firm. Repeat with the remaining four. Keep warm, wrapped in a clean tea towel.

4 Blanch the cabbage in a pan of boiling salted water, then drain well.

5 Heat the butter in a sauté pan and add the garlic, cook for 1 minute, then add the cream and bring to the boil. Toss in the cabbage, season well and stir-fry for 2–3 minutes until the cabbage is glazed with the cream and still very slightly crisp. Butter the scones.

6 To serve, place a hot buttered scone on each plate. Stir the smoked salmon into the cabbage and spoon over the scones. Top with another scone, scatter with chopped parsley and serve.

85 Seared Salmon Niçoise

Informal supper
Preparation time 35 minutes
Serves 4

350 g (12 oz) small waxy potatoes (such as Anya)

175 g (6 oz) fine green beans, topped and tailed

2 large ripe tomatoes, quartered

6 tinned anchovy fillets, rinsed and dried

50 g (1/3 cup) black olives (Greek-style are good for this dish)

3 hard-boiled eggs, peeled and quartered

450 g (1 lb) salmon fillet, cut into medallions (see pages 10–11)

crusty bread, to serve

FOR THE DRESSING:

6 tablespoons olive oil

2 tablespoons white wine vinegar or lemon juice

1/2 teaspoon Dijon mustard

2 tablespoons salted capers, rinsed and drained

3 tablespoons chopped mixed herbs (parsley, basil, chives, tarragon)

freshly ground sea salt and freshly ground black pepper

It's hard to improve on a classic dish. And I'm not claiming that using salmon instead of tuna in this recipe is an improvement, but salmon does work so well with all the Niçoise ingredients – potatoes, eggs and tomato – that the dish could have been created with a nice piece of seared salmon in mind.

1 Boil the potatoes in salted water for 15 minutes or until tender, adding the green beans about 4 minutes before the potatoes are ready.

2 Whisk all the dressing ingredients together and set aside.

3 Drain the potatoes and beans and slice the potatoes thickly. Put the potato slices and beans into a bowl and pour over a splash of dressing while the vegetables are still hot. Then mix in the tomatoes, anchovies and olives. Tip out on to a large serving platter and scatter the quartered eggs over the top.

4 Pat the salmon dry and dry-fry or sear in batches in a very hot pan for 1 minute on each side. Lift out of the pan and place on to the middle of the salad.

5 Quickly heat up the remaining dressing in a small pan and, when boiling, pour over the salad. Serve with loads of crusty bread.

86 Seared Salmon and Beet with Mustard Dressing

Informal supper
Preparation time 25 minutes
Serves 4

450 g (1 lb) small whole beet, scrubbed and trimmed

4 tablespoons olive oil

8 garlic cloves, skins left on

2 tablespoons balsamic vinegar

freshly ground sea salt and freshly ground black pepper

2 tablespoons wholegrain mustard

350 g (12 oz) salmon fillet, cut into medallions (see pages 10-11)

a squeeze of lemon juice

2 tablespoons chopped fresh chives

Salmon has a natural affinity with beet and I've used the partnership successfully in a number of dishes. This is one of my favorites at home. My wife, Holly, grows an Italian variegated variety – 'Barbabietola Di Chioggi' – which I normally use in this dish. It has several advantages: it looks pretty with its purple-and-white striped interior, it doesn't stain your hands when you prepare it, and it tastes fab – a very sweet and clean flavor. Holly also assures me that it's easy to grow. If you can't find it, the normal stuff is fine, but wear rubber gloves when preparing it to prevent your hands getting stained – or you could cheat and use precooked beet for simplicity.

1 Preheat the oven to 200°C/400°F.

2 Peel the beet and cut into quarters, or sixths if the beet is large. Pour 3 tablespoons of the olive oil into a small roasting pan, then add the beet and whole garlic cloves. Toss well to coat with the oil, sprinkle over the balsamic vinegar and season with salt and pepper.

3 Roast in the oven for 20–25 minutes, basting occasionally. When the beet is cooked, add the mustard and toss well to coat.

4 Heat a large frying pan until very hot. Add the remaining oil, then flash-fry the salmon in batches for about 1–2 minutes on one side only. Quickly lift the slices on to a baking sheet and season with a little lemon juice, salt and pepper.

5 Add the chives to the beet and pile on to four warmed plates, making sure the garlic is evenly distributed. Place a pile of seared salmon medallions on each plate of beet and spoon over any pan juices.

87 Seared Salmon with Wilted Greens and Chili Oil

Quick and easy
Preparation time 25 minutes
Serves 4

3 tablespoons sunflower oil

1 garlic clove, finely chopped

1 zucchini, thinly sliced lengthways

50 g (2 oz) fine green beans

85 g (3 oz) bok choi

115 g (4 oz) fresh young spinach, washed

3 tablespoons chopped fresh coriander

juice of 1 lime

1–2 tablespoons soy sauce (preferably Kikkoman's)

freshly ground sea salt and freshly ground black pepper

4 × 115 g (4 oz) salmon escalopes (see page 10)

a squeeze of lemon juice

3 tablespoons chili oil

This is a quick, easy and healthy dish, which I often prepare at home. You can vary the greens, choosing from zucchini, sugar peas, bok choi, spinach, Chinese greens, Savoy cabbage, kale, mustard leaves and so on. Always add the thicker, chunkier vegetables to the pan first (zucchini or Savoy cabbage), followed by the delicate ones (spinach or bok choi). That way, all the vegetables are cooked to perfection together. I normally make my own chili oil (see below), but recently I've been impressed by the quality of some of the chili oils found in the speciality section of larger supermarkets.

1 Heat half the oil in a large sauté pan or wok, add the garlic and cook for 30 seconds. Add the zucchini and beans, and gently stir-fry for a further minute until starting to color, then add the bok choi. When the greens are starting to wilt, add the spinach, coriander, lime juice, soy sauce and seasoning, toss well and cook for a couple of minutes until wilted down.

2 Meanwhile, fry the salmon escalopes in the remaining oil in a non-stick frying pan over a searing heat for 1–2 minutes. Turn out on to a plate cooked-side up, and season with salt, pepper and a squeeze of lemon juice.

3 Divide the greens between four serving plates, making a nice pile in the center. Carefully place the salmon on top, drizzle the chili oil around and over the salmon and serve.

Chili Oil

This mega mega spicy oil can be made well in advance and keeps for ages. Used sparingly, chili oil imparts a wonderful glow to many dishes. Slice 225 g (8 oz) ripe fresh red chilies in half lengthways and place in a saucepan. Pour over 1 liter (1³/₄ pints) sunflower oil, put the pan on the burner and bring to the boil. Simmer gently for 5 minutes, remove from the heat and allow to cool (this takes about 2 hours). Once cooled, transfer the whole lot to a plastic tub with a lid and store in a cool place for 2–3 weeks. After this time, pour the oil through a sieve to remove the chilies before using it (or your oil will just get too hot). I usually keep the chili oil in an old olive oil bottle, but remember to label it well. A skull and crossbones will suffice!

88 Roasted Salmon with Fennel, Celery and Black Olives

Informal supper
Preparation time 20 minutes
Serves 4–6

1 kg (2 lb 4 oz) whole salmon or piece or joint of salmon on the bone, scaled and gutted

a few sprigs of fresh rosemary

2 large fennel bulbs

4 celery sticks

150 ml (^{2}/$_3$ cup) decent olive oil

juice of 1 lemon

1 tablespoon dried oregano

3 tablespoons chopped fresh parsley

freshly ground sea salt and freshly ground black pepper

12 black olives, pitted (optional)

150 ml (^{2}/$_3$ cup) dry white wine

boiled new potatoes, to serve (optional)

This is a particularly good way to cook a large piece of salmon as, not only does it allow the Italian-influenced flavors to infuse themselves into the fish, but the vegetables are also cooked at the same time. The salmon is equally good served hot or cold.

1 Preheat the oven to 220°C/425°F.

2 Wash the salmon inside and out, making sure you've cleaned out all the dark blood near to the backbone. Fill the cavity with small sprigs of rosemary.

3 Cut the fennel bulbs in half lengthways and trim off the woody stalks. Trim away any green fronds and set these aside. Cut out the hard core and slice the fennel roughly. Slice the celery roughly. Blanch the vegetables in boiling salted water for 3–5 minutes to soften, then drain.

4 Whisk the oil, lemon juice, herbs, salt and pepper together in a medium bowl and pour over the fennel and celery. Toss well to coat. Spread this over the base of a shallow ovenproof dish big enough to take the salmon. Lay the salmon on top of the fennel mixture, tuck in the olives (if using) around the fish and pour over the wine.

5 Bake in the oven for 30 minutes. Baste the salmon with the released juices from time to time and give the vegetables an occasional stir. Remove from the oven, cover the salmon with a piece of foil and leave for 5 minutes to 'set.' Uncover and serve, lifting off the skin and easing the salmon off the bone into nice flakes. Serve with a pile of the vegetables and perhaps a few new potatoes.

Vegetables, greens and salads

89 Char-grilled Salmon with Roast Vegetables and Pesto

Smart entertaining
Preparation time 40 minutes
Serves 4

1 medium eggplant, sliced lengthways into 4–6 slices

freshly ground sea salt and freshly ground black pepper

1 quantity Pesto (see page 13)

2–3 tablespoons olive oil, plus extra for brushing

1 long red pepper, halved and seeded

1 long yellow pepper, halved and seeded

225 g (8 oz) baby new potatoes, thickly sliced

2 zucchini, sliced lengthways into 4 long slices

1 fennel bulb, quartered

1 red onion, sliced into 6 segments

4 × 140 g (5 oz) salmon fillets

sunflower oil, for brushing

juice of 1 lemon

To get the best from your grill pan, it is important that it is properly seasoned. One method of doing this is to place the pan over a medium heat, then wipe it every 5–10 minutes with a cloth soaked in vegetable oil for about an hour, until it has darkened.

1 Put the eggplant slices in a colander, salt them well and leave for 30 minutes. This removes excess liquid and gives the cooked eggplant a tender texture and flavor.

2 Dilute the pesto with the olive oil until quite runny. Set aside.

3 Heat a ribbed grill pan until very hot. Rinse the eggplant well and then pat dry. Brush all the vegetables, including the potatoes, with plenty of olive oil and season on both sides, then grill a few at a time until well colored and tender. Once the vegetables are all cooked, set aside and keep warm.

4 Wipe the grill pan clean and reheat until medium hot. Lightly brush the salmon fillets with sunflower oil and season. Place them on the grill. Cook for 2 minutes, then rotate the fillets through 90 degrees to give a nice criss-cross effect. Cook for another minute, turn over and repeat. When cooked, squeeze over a little lemon juice.

5 Place a pile of the roast vegetables in the center of four warmed serving plates. Place the char-grilled salmon on top, spoon around the Pesto and serve.

90 Baked Salmon, Zucchini Fritters and Roasted Long Peppers

Smart entertaining
Preparation time 35 minutes
Serves 4

40 g (3 tablespoons) butter

4 × 140 g (5 oz) salmon fillets

juice of 1 lemon

freshly ground sea salt and freshly ground black pepper

4 long red 'Ramiro' peppers, ends cut off and seeds scooped out

2 tablespoons olive oil, plus extra for drizzling

FOR THE ZUCCHINI FRITTERS:

3 medium zucchini, coarsely grated

1 1/2 teaspoons freshly ground sea salt

2 medium eggs, separated

150 ml (2/3 cup) 35% cream

85 g (1/2 cup) all-purpose flour

2 green onions, finely chopped

sunflower oil, for shallow-frying

These fritters are more like zucchini pancakes and are quite rich. They need only the addition of a nice piece of baked salmon and a roasted pepper to create a colorful and satisfying main course. I like to use the long 'Ramiro' peppers, available in larger supermarkets. If there are any juices left from roasting the peppers, pour these over the salmon.

1 Preheat the oven to 200°C/400°F.

2 Heavily butter a shallow baking dish and add the salmon fillets. Squeeze over half the lemon juice, dot generously with the remaining butter and season. Set aside.

3 Place the peppers on a roasting tray, coat with olive oil and bake in the oven for 20–25 minutes, until the peppers are softened and starting to blacken. Part-way into the cooking time put the salmon into the oven as well and bake for 7–10 minutes. Once cooked, remove the salmon and the peppers, cover with foil and keep warm.

4 Meanwhile, make the zucchini fritters. Mix the grated zucchini with a teaspoon of salt and leave to drain in a sieve for 5 minutes. Rinse off the salt, squeeze out the excess water and dry well on paper towel.

5 Whisk the egg yolks and cream together in a bowl and then whisk in the flour to make a smooth batter. Stir in the green onions and the zucchini. Whisk the egg whites and half a teaspoon of salt together in a separate bowl until they form soft peaks – make sure they don't get too stiff or they won't blend into the rest of the mixture. Fold a large tablespoon of the egg whites into the zucchini mixture to loosen it slightly and then gently fold in the remainder.

7 Heat about 1 cm (1/2 inch) of sunflower oil in a large frying pan, until a little zucchini mixture will instantly sizzle when it hits the oil. Drop in two large spoonfuls of the batter, spacing them a little apart, and fry for 3–4 minutes on each side over a medium heat until golden. Drain on paper towel and keep warm in the bottom of the oven beside the salmon and peppers. Make the other two fritters.

9 To serve, place a zucchini fritter in the center of each warmed serving plate and top with a whole roast pepper. Place a baked salmon fillet on top, squeeze over a little more lemon juice and drizzle with olive oil.

91 Grilled Salmon with Peas, Lettuce and Bacon

Quick and easy
Preparation time 25 minutes
Serves 4

4 × 175 g (6 oz) salmon steaks or darnes (see pages 10–11)

65 g (¹/₃ cup) butter

freshly ground sea salt and freshly ground black pepper

2 × 130 g (4.5 oz) packets lardons (*cubetti di pancetta*)

2 Little Gem lettuces, finely shredded

200 ml (³/₄ cup) vegetable, fish or chicken stock

225 g (1¹/₂ cups) fresh or frozen peas

2 tablespoons 35% cream (optional)

3 tablespoons chopped fresh parsley

freshly squeezed lemon juice

Peas, lettuce and sweet bacon are perfect with simply grilled salmon. This is my version of a French classic, but cooked for less time to keep the vibrant spring flavors. A couple of tablespoons of cream can be added to the vegetables with the peas to give a super-deluxe version!

1 Preheat the grill for at least 10 minutes. Remove any 'pin bones' from the steaks. Melt 25 g (2 tablespoons) of the butter in a small pan and brush over the salmon. Season generously. Line a grill pan with foil, then place the salmon under the grill and grill for about 3–4 minutes per side (take care not to overcook the fish). When it's cooked, cover and keep warm.

2 While the salmon is cooking, heat a frying pan until quite hot and add the lardons. Turn down the heat and cook the lardons for 2–3 minutes, stirring, until the fat starts to run and they begin to take on a bit of color.

3 Add the shredded lettuces and stir for a minute to coat with the fat from the lardons. Pour in the stock, season and bring to the boil, then turn down the heat and simmer, uncovered, for 3 minutes.

4 Next, add the peas, cream (if using) and parsley, give the pan a good shake while it comes to the boil, and add the remaining butter. Let this melt into the 'stew,' simmer for 2 minutes, then taste and add a squeeze or two of lemon juice to lift it. Serve with the grilled steaks.

92 Smoked Salmon, Cherry Tomato and Asparagus Pizza

Informal supper
Preparation time 15 minutes, plus rising time
Makes 2 × 23–25 cm (9–10 inch) thin-crust pizzas

350 g (2½ cups) all-purpose white flour, plus extra for dusting

15 g (2 tablespoons) fresh yeast, 1 tablespoon dried active baking yeast, or 1 packet easy-blend yeast

2 tablespoons olive oil, plus extra for brushing and drizzling

a pinch of salt

FOR THE TOPPING:

150 ml (⅔ cup) fresh tomato sauce, or equal quantities of tomato ketchup and tomato paste mixed with a pinch of cayenne

175 g (6 oz) fresh asparagus, trimmed, blanched for 1 minute and refreshed

12 cherry tomatoes, halved

1 ball mozzarella cheese, thinly sliced

freshly ground sea salt and freshly ground black pepper

3 tablespoons grated Parmesan cheese

olive oil or Chili Oil (see page 123), for drizzling

115 g (4 oz) sliced smoked salmon

1 fresh red chili, finely sliced

Without the fierce heat of a wood-burning oven, you'll never exactly recreate the flavor and texture of a Neapolitan pizza. However, by having your oven turned up to maximum and preheating a heavy baking sheet (or better still, a terracotta pizza stone, sold in most good kitchen shops) near the top of the oven, you will be able to produce a pizza of a quality that will more than repay the effort that goes into doing it yourself. Remember: the more filling you add to the pizza, the longer it will take to cook.

1 Sift the flour into a large bowl. Crumble in the fresh yeast (follow the packet instructions for dried or sprinkle in the easy-blend) and rub in with your fingers. Make a well in the center and add 250 ml (1 cup) hand-hot water, the olive oil and a good pinch of salt. Mix with your hands until the dough comes together. Tip out on to a floured surface, wash and dry your hands (the dough won't stick this way) and knead for 10 minutes until smooth and elastic. The dough should be quite soft, but if too soft to handle, add a bit more flour; if not soft enough, add more water – make this often enough and you'll soon get the feel! Place the dough in a clean, oiled bowl, cover with a damp tea towel and leave to rise until doubled – about 1 hour.

2 Meanwhile, preheat the oven to its highest setting – the oven and baking sheets or pizza stone will need to heat for at least 30 minutes.

3 Punch down the risen dough and cut in two. Roll each piece out as thinly as you can, ensuring the dough is well floured underneath, and place on two baking sheets.

4 Spread the pizzas with tomato sauce almost to the edges. Scatter the asparagus and tomatoes over the sauce. Dot with the mozzarella, season and sprinkle with Parmesan. Drizzle over the olive or Chili Oil. Leave for 5 minutes to puff up slightly.

5 Either place the two pizzas on the two oven shelves, bake for 10–15 minutes, then swap them around, bake for a further 10 minutes and serve immediately with the crumpled smoked salmon and scattered chili on top. Or, if using a baking stone, you'll have to cook the pizzas one after the other. Slide the first pizza on to the hot baking stone as quickly as you can (this is tricky – especially if your dough isn't floured enough). Bake for 15–20 minutes, then remove the first pizza and replace with the second. Start eating the first straight away – pizza doesn't hang around!

93 Salmon Baked in Filo with Spinach and Feta

Informal supper
Preparation time 45 minutes
Serves 4

2 × 200 g (8 oz) packets washed spinach leaves

freshly ground sea salt and freshly ground black pepper

a little freshly grated nutmeg

grated rind and juice of $1/2$ lemon

8 large sheets Greek filo pastry

4 × 140 g (5 oz) salmon fillets

175 g (6 oz) feta cheese, crumbled

melted butter, for brushing

dressed salad, to serve

The nicest thing about this dish is the contrast of textures: crunchy pastry, crumbly cheese, soft spinach and meltingly tender salmon. The next best thing is that it can all be made up in advance and kept in the fridge until it's time to put the pastry parcels in the oven.

1 Preheat the oven to 220°C/425°F.

2 Cook the spinach with a couple of tablespoons of water until just wilted. Drain and squeeze out the excess moisture. Roughly chop and season with salt, pepper, nutmeg to taste and the lemon rind and juice.

3 Take two sheets of filo pastry together (keeping the rest under a damp, not wet, tea towel) and set a salmon fillet about one-third of the way up from the short end. Cover the fillet with a quarter of the spinach, press down gently, then top with a quarter of the feta. Flick the short end of the pastry up over the salmon, flip the long edges inwards, then carefully roll the fillet up the length of the pastry. Brush with melted butter and set on a baking sheet. Repeat with the remaining ingredients to make four filo parcels in all.

4 Bake for 15 minutes until crisp and golden and serve immediately with a big bowl of well-dressed salad.

94 Poached Salmon with Garden Salad

Quick and easy
Preparation time 10 minutes
Serves 2

115 g (4 oz) mixed young salad leaves

25 g (1 oz) rocket and basil leaves, mixed

50 g (1/2 cup) fresh or frozen peas, cooked

2 × 140 g (5 oz) salmon fillets

juice of 1 lemon

1 ripe avocado, peeled, pitted and diced into 1 cm (1/2 inch) chunks

6 cherry tomatoes, halved

1 small carrot, peeled and shaved into ribbons

freshly ground sea salt and freshly ground black pepper

2 tablespoons extra virgin olive oil

2 teaspoons balsamic vinegar

The perfect salad should have a good mixture of leaves of different colors and flavors – I like about equal quantities sweet, bitter and peppery. Then you need to add a bit of drama by the way of crunch, which is where the carrot and peas come in, and finally some softer texture with the avocado and tomato (both of which must be ripe). Having prepared this heavenly mixture, you need only the simplest of dressings – good olive oil and lemon juice with a seasoning of freshly ground sea salt and freshly ground black pepper is perfect.

1 First prepare the salad. Pick over the salad and herb leaves and place them in a shallow bowl with the peas. Keep them covered and refrigerated until you're ready to serve.

2 Lay the salmon fillets in a shallow pan and pour in enough water to cover. Squeeze in the lemon juice and then slowly bring up to just below boiling point. Barely simmer for 4 minutes until the salmon is *just* cooked. Lift out of the pan, drain well and place each fillet on a serving plate.

3 Take the salad leaves out of the fridge, add the avocado, tomatoes and carrot ribbons and season with salt and pepper. Drizzle with the oil, then the balsamic vinegar, and toss to coat. Don't soak the salad in dressing: it's important simply to coat the leaves. Divide the salad between the two plates of salmon and serve.

95 Olive-oil-poached Salmon with Celeriac and Crispy Bacon

Smart entertaining
Preparation time 30 minutes
Serves 4

sunflower oil, for deep-frying

4 slices of Parma ham

700 ml (2 ³/4 cups) olive oil

4 x 140 g (5 oz) salmon fillets

FOR THE CELERIAC PURÉE:

225 g (8 oz) celeriac

25 g (2 tablespoons) butter

2–3 tablespoons milk

freshly ground sea salt and freshly ground black pepper

Poaching salmon in olive oil might sound like a totally unjustifiable extravagance, but this cooking method does produce a salmon fillet with a unique flavor and the most melting texture. If you keep the cooking oil in the fridge and use it several times for poaching, it starts to make some sort of financial sense. Celeriac purée has a unique flavor and silky texture that complements the poached salmon, and acts as vegetable and sauce – all you need for gastronomic fireworks are some slices of crispy deep-fried Parma ham. This is definitely a special occasion dish!

1 To make the purée, peel the celeriac, then cut it into chunks. Cook in boiling salted water for 15–20 minutes, until the celeriac is very tender. Drain well, then put the hot celeriac into a food processor with the butter and milk and whizz for 3–4 minutes until very smooth. Check the seasoning. This can be made the day before and gently reheated with a knob of butter.

2 Pour 2 cm (³/4 inch) of sunflower oil into a medium-sized saucepan or electric deep-fat fryer and heat to 180°C/350°F (use a cooking thermometer if necessary). Deep-fry the Parma ham slices, two at a time, for about 30 seconds until nice and crisp. Drain them on paper towel and set aside.

3 Put the olive oil into a medium saucepan. Heat up to 50°C/122°F (again you may need a cooking thermometer for this). Slip in the salmon fillets – the oil should completely cover them. Poach – that is, cook at this temperature and no higher – for 10–12 minutes, depending on the thickness of the fillets. Then lift out and drain on paper towel.

4 Meanwhile, reheat the celeriac purée. To serve, put some celeriac purée in the center of each plate, lay a salmon fillet on top and finish with a crunchy piece of Parma ham.

96 Salmon Rarebit with Sauce Vierge

Informal supper
Preparation time 20 minutes
Serves 4

350 g (3 cups) mature Cheddar cheese, grated

85 ml (¹/₃ cup) milk

2 tablespoons all-purpose flour

25 g (¹/₄ cup) fresh white breadcrumbs

1 teaspoon English mustard powder

a few drops of Worcestershire sauce

freshly ground sea salt and freshly ground black pepper

1 egg, beaten with 1 egg yolk

4 × 115 g (4 oz) chunky smoked salmon fillets

1 quantity Sauce Vierge (see page 14), to serve

I love the sharp, cheesy flavor of this rarebit topping (make sure you use a good-quality, mature Cheddar) on top of a piece of baked salmon. All it needs to complete the dish is a spoonful of Sauce Vierge (see page 14). I like to finish the rarebit under a hot grill to give it a nice, golden color. The rarebit topping will make enough for about 12 servings, but it keeps for several days in the fridge and can be used to top a variety of different things, even toast.

1 Put the cheddar cheese into a pan and add the milk. Slowly melt them together over a low heat, but do not allow to boil, as this will separate the cheese.

2 When the mixture is smooth, stir in the flour, breadcrumbs, mustard and a few drops of Worcestershire sauce and cook for a few minutes, stirring over a low heat until the mixture comes away from the sides of the pan into a big lump. Beat in the seasoning and eggs and leave to cool, then chill for an hour or so.

3 Preheat the oven to 180°C/350°F and the grill to medium. Arrange the salmon fillets in a buttered flameproof dish. Take the cheese mixture out of the fridge and use 4 heaped tablespoons (keep the rest in a plastic bag for another time), patting each one out to fit the size and shape of each salmon fillet. Lay the rarebit pieces on top of the salmon.

4 Bake the salmon in the oven for 5–7 minutes, then put under the grill until golden brown. Serve with the Sauce Vierge.

97 Orange and Coriander Marinated Salmon

Prepare in advance
Preparation time 20 minutes
Serves 6 as a starter, 4 as a main dish

150 ml (²/₃ cup) olive oil, plus extra for frying

4 × 175 g (6 oz) salmon fillets, skinned

1 tablespoon coriander seeds

6 green onions, shredded

3 garlic cloves, thinly sliced

2 fresh red chilies, seeded and sliced

3 fresh bay leaves

2 tablespoons chopped fresh coriander

finely pared rind and juice of 1 orange

3 tablespoons dry white wine

3 tablespoons white wine vinegar

freshly ground sea salt and freshly ground black pepper

bitter leafy salad and crusty bread, to serve

In the Latin American world this dish is known as *escabeche*, meaning 'pickled fish.' The fish is normally coated in flour and fried before being marinated in olive oil, vinegar and herbs and spices.
I have simplified this by pan-frying the salmon without coating in flour – it tastes and looks much cleaner! Serve it at room temperature, not straight out of the fridge. Instead of using fresh coriander, you could try fresh marjoram or oregano, or even freeze-dried oregano.

1 Wipe a non-stick frying pan with a little olive oil and fry the salmon fillets for 3–4 minutes on each side until just cooked through. Remove from the pan and lay in a single layer in a non-metallic dish.

2 Wipe out the pan again until clean and dry-fry the coriander seeds until they begin to release their aroma. Tip out of the pan and lightly crush.

3 Mix the crushed coriander seeds with all the other ingredients and pour over the salmon. Cover with plastic wrap and leave to marinate in the fridge for at least 12 hours. Serve the salmon fillets at room temperature with a couple of tablespoons of marinade, a bitter leafy salad and plenty of good crusty bread to mop up.

98 Cajun Spiced Salmon with Cucumber Salad

Informal supper
Preparation time 20 minutes
Serves 6

6 × 175 g (6 oz) thick salmon fillets, unskinned

3 tablespoons paprika powder

1 teaspoon dried chili flakes

1/2 teaspoon dried thyme

1/2 teaspoon dried oregano

1 teaspoon black peppercorns

1/2 teaspoon cumin seeds

2 teaspoons freshly ground sea salt, plus extra for sprinkling

3 tablespoons olive oil, plus extra to serve

FOR THE CUCUMBER SALAD:

2 cucumbers

1 large garlic clove, very finely chopped

1 tablespoon lemon or lime juice

1 long thin red chili, seeded and finely chopped (optional)

2 tablespoons chopped fresh coriander

I'm very fond of the contrast of the hot spicy salmon and the clean crisp cucumber salad in this dish. There may seem to be a lot of ingredients in the Cajun spice mix, but don't let this put you off as you can make a large batch that keeps well in an airtight jar for future Cajun cooking.

1 Score the skin of the salmon with a sharp knife and set aside.

2 Put the paprika, chili flakes, thyme, oregano, black peppercorns, cumin seeds and salt into a mortar or coffee grinder and grind to a fine powder. Sprinkle over the base of a large plate.

3 Brush the skin of the salmon with some of the olive oil and then dip only the skin side into the salt and spices, making sure that each piece is coated with an even layer.

4 To make the cucumber salad, peel the cucumbers, cut them in half lengthways and scoop out the seeds with a melon-baller or teaspoon. Cut them lengthways into long, thin shreds, using a potato peeler, and then dry well in a clean tea towel. Set aside in the fridge to chill until needed.

5 Heat a smooth, cast-iron grill until hot. Add a little olive oil and then the salmon, skin-side down. Cook over a medium heat for about 5 minutes until the skin is nice and crisp. Brush the flesh of the salmon pieces with the remaining oil, turn the fish over and cook for another 2–3 minutes until just cooked though. Lift the salmon on to a baking sheet straight away so that it doesn't continue to cook.

6 Add the garlic, lemon or lime juice, chili, if using, coriander and a pinch of salt to the cucumber and toss together well. Pile the salad in the center of each plate and place a piece of salmon on top. Drizzle around a little more olive oil and serve.

99 Salmon Tortilla and Guacamole

Informal supper
Preparation time 15 minutes
Serves 4

350 g (12 oz) middle cut salmon fillet, cut into medallions (see pages 10–11)

sour cream, to serve

limes, to serve (optional)

FOR THE GUACAMOLE:

2 ripe avocados, halved, pitted and peeled

juice of 1–2 limes (depending on juiciness)

1/2 onion, grated, or 1 garlic clove creamed with a little salt

1 fresh green chili, seeded and very finely chopped

2 tablespoons chopped fresh coriander, plus extra to serve

freshly ground sea salt and freshly ground black pepper

FOR THE TORTILLAS:

1 teaspoon freshly ground sea salt

225 g (1 1/2 cups) all-purpose flour

2 tablespoons vegetable oil

150 ml (2/3 cup) warm water

This is a really simple recipe and can be even easier if you use ready-made tortillas – quick, but not nearly as satisfying as making your own. Ripe avocados are essential; look out for the ready-to-eat varieties available in some supermarkets. I've specified sour cream here, but crème fraîche or whipped cream with lemon juice folded through work just as well.

1 To make the guacamole, put all the ingredients into a bowl and roughly mash with a fork. Cover and set aside.

2 Put the tortilla ingredients in a food processor with 150 ml (2/3 cup) warm water and blitz for a minute until just combined. Turn out and knead the dough until smooth. Divide into eight pieces, shape into smooth balls and keep covered with a warm, damp tea towel.

3 Roll each ball out on a floured surface as thinly as you can – they should be about 23 cm (9 inches) wide. Stack up between pieces of baking parchment while you heat a large, heavy frying pan. Cook each tortilla for about a minute on each side – small bubbles will appear on the surface when it is ready to turn. Stack them up in a clean tea towel to keep warm.

4 Flash-fry the salmon medallions in batches in a non-stick frying pan for about 1 minute. Serve the salmon from the pan with the pile of tortillas, the bowl of guacamole, a bowl of sour cream and extra coriander for each person to make up their own tortilla. Extra limes would be good, too!

Seared Medallions of Salmon with Hot Pepper Marmalade

Smart entertaining
Preparation time 40 minutes for marmalade
Serves 4

350 g (12 oz) salmon fillet, cut into medallions (see pages 10–11)

freshly squeezed lemon juice

freshly ground sea salt and freshly ground black pepper

4 tablespoons crème fraîche or sour cream and a handful of rocket leaves, to serve

FOR THE HOT PEPPER MARMALADE:

1 medium red onion, finely chopped

2 garlic cloves, finely chopped

1 teaspoon ground coriander

2 tablespoons olive oil, plus extra for frying

2 red peppers, seeded and chopped or cut into thin strips

2.5 cm (1 inch) piece fresh ginger, peeled and finely grated

2 long thin red chilies, finely chopped (seeds and all)

100 ml (6 tablespoons) red wine vinegar

40 g (6 tablespoons) soft light brown sugar

This is a cracking combination of hot and sour, sweet and salty. The most complicated part of the dish is making the hot pepper marmalade. However, as this benefits from being made in advance, the actual preparation of the dish is relatively simple. The secret of success is in cooking the salmon so that it has a nice, crispy crust with soft, underdone salmon below. The crème fraîche adds not only acidity, but also a cool temperature contrast.

1 To make the hot pepper marmalade, sweat the onion, garlic and ground coriander in the olive oil for about 5 minutes until soft and golden. Add the chopped red peppers, ginger and chilies and cook over a low heat for another 10 minutes until soft. Add the vinegar and sugar, bring up to a simmer and leave to cook gently for 20 minutes, giving the mixture an occasional stir every now and then. The final mixture should be thick and jam-like.

2 Heat a large frying pan until very hot. Add 1 tablespoon oil, then flash-fry the salmon in batches for about 1–2 minutes on one side only. Quickly lift the slices on to a baking sheet and season with a little lemon juice, salt and pepper.

3 Arrange a pile of salmon on each plate and spoon some hot pepper marmalade around it. Add a spoonful of crème fraîche and surround with rocket leaves.